A Study Investigating the Effectiveness of the No Child Left Behind Law on special need

students and the use of technology.

Vincient A.Spears

Strayer University

Research Methods

Table of Contents

Abstract

The Individuals with Disabilities Education Improvement Act (IDEA) of 2006 and the   No Child Left Behind Act (U.S. Department of Education, 2001) legislation mandate that students with disabilities be taught to the same high standards as students without disabilities. E-IEP for special needs students like FAS/FAE was created by integrating assistive technology in the classroom (www.iowa-iep.net). Special education, more than other areas of education, is governed by laws and policies. This means that teachers, administrators, and special education technology specialists must be well versed in federal and state laws, policies, and procedures. To learn more about the legal and policy foundations of the field of special education technology, consult the following resources: Blackhurt (1997), Blackhurst and Edyburn (2000), U.S Department of Education (2000). Vincient A.S pears thinks that technologies have help his daughter cope in school and help to learned reading technologies software, activities and construct activities. E-IEP for special needs students like FAS/FAE was created by integrating assistive technology in the classroom (www.iowa-iep.net). Special education, more than other areas of education, is governed by laws and policies. This means that teachers, administrators, and special education technology specialists must be well versed in federal and state laws, policies, and procedures. To learn more about the legal and policy foundations of the field of special education technology, consult the following resources: Blackhurt (1997), Blackhurst and Edyburn (2000).

The following U.S. laws promote the use of technology by individuals with disabilities:

1. The Technology-Related Assistance Act for Individuals with Disabilities (Public Law 100-407), passed in 1988, provides funding for statewide systems and services to provide assistive technology devices and services to individuals with disabilities.

2. Reauthorization of the Individuals with Disabilities Education Act (IDEA) in 1997 (Public Law 105-17) mandates that every individualized education program (IEP) team " consider" assistive technology when planning the education program of an individual with a disability. The most current reauthorization in 2004 contain no new technology information, but serves reemphasize to schools the importance of academic achievement by students with disabilities and the need to help each student meet achievement goals.

Diverse learners or FAS/FAE students use newspapers, periodicals Dora's dolls and software, DVD, or archived document to explore topic belong or in addition to that covered by other students or memory games. New technologies also increase teacher capability to adapt classrooms to accommodate special-needs students (www.prenhall.com/specialed).At the Technology for Education website (www.http://tfenc.com), teachers and parents can search by category, vendor, or product name for hundreds of assistive tools.SPAN (Student Parent Access Network) is use help parents with their progress and to learn about computer and networking (www.wcpss.net). As computers become increasingly popular in today's homes, teachers have greater opportunities to communicate with students and parents.

1. Appropriate Educational Placement can make all the difference in a child's success. Many children with FAS/FAE require special education services due to significant learning disablities,emotional and behavioral diffulties or multiple handicapping conditions and special

technologies like Alternate Keyboards, Easy-to Read Screens, Electronic Point Devices. 2. Individual assessments in Speech/Language, Occupational Therapy, and cognitive functioning are necessary in establishing a child's strengths and deficits. Other evaluations which may be helpful are: Psychiatric, neurological and physical therapy. FAS/FAE use Quicktionary Reading Pen (WizCom) and eReader help students' communication. For individuals with moderate and severe cognitive disabilities, considerable effort is devoted to ensuring that they acquire daily living skills such as personal hygiene, shopping (Wissick, 1999), and use of public transportation. In addition, software is available to help teach functional skills such as money management (Browder & Grasso, 1999). 3. Diverse learners or FAS/FAE students use newspapers, periodicals Dora's dolls and software, DVD, or archived document to explore topic beong or in addition to that covered by other students or memory games. New technologies also increase teacher capability to adapt classrooms to accommodate special-needs students (www.prenhall.com/specialed).At the Technology for Education website (www.http://tfenc.com), teachers and parents can search by category, vendor, or product name for hundreds of assistive tools. SPAN (Student Parent Access Network) is use help parents with their progress and to learn about computer and networking (www.wcpss.net). As computers become increasingly popular in today's homes, teachers have greater opportunities to communicate with students and parents.

IEP or Individual assessments in Speech/Language, Occupational Therapy, and cognitive functioning are necessary in establishing a child's strengths and deficits. Other evaluations which may be helpful are: Psychiatric, neurological and physical therapy. FAS/FAE use Quicktionary

Reading Pen (WizCom) and eReader help students' communication. For individuals with moderate and severe cognitive disabilities, considerable effort is devoted to ensuring that they acquire daily living skills such as personal hygiene, shopping (Wissick, 1999), and use of public transportation. In addition, software is available to help teach functional skills such as money management (Browder & Grasso, 1999). The writer's adoptive daughter likes to create story with e-toy story book and special educational software.

The child's educational plan should be developed based on the child's individual needs. Considerable effort has been devoted to identifying the knowledge and skills needed by teachers (Lahm& Nickels, 1999) and specialist (Lahm, 2000) to use technology in special education. Individuals can use the NETS competency statements to document their experience, knowledge, and skills in their own teaching portfolio. According to U.S. Department of Education (2000),Despite the efforts on the part of most universities to improve the preparation of teachers to use technology in the classroom, most teachers begin their career with minimal experience using technology in way that (1) enhance their own productivity, (2) enhance the effectiveness of instruction and the success of all students, and/ or (3) enable them to acquire and use assistive technology for students in need of performance support. The common three-credit course, first developed in the 1980s, continues to be the norm for preparing teachers; unfortunately, it is generally inadequate in exploiting the power and possibilities that technology offers.

Another issue regarding the adequacy of the training in special education technology centers on the use of interdisciplinary teams for evaluating the need for assistive technology and decision making in the selection of appropriate device and services. The current assistive technology delivery and system was originally developed to respond to the needs of students with low-incidence disabilities (approximately 1.4 million students in the United States).

References:

Addison, J.T. (1992). Urie Bronfenbrenner. Human Ecology, 20(2), 16-20.

Armbruster, B., Lehr, F., Osborn, J.B. 2003, A Child Becomes A Reader K-3, Second Edition

BAS; Wilson&Sloan, 2000) "

Desimone, L., Finn-Stevenson, M., and Henrich, C. (200) Whole School Reform In A Low-Income African American Community: The Effects Of The CoZi Model On Teachers, Parents, And Students. Urban Education, 35 (3), 269-323.

Kleinfeld, Judith, and Wescott, Siobhan.Fantastic Antone Succeeds! University of Alaska Press.1993

Mattingley, D.J., Prislin, R., Mckenzie, T.L., Rodriquez, and J.L., and Kayzar, B. 2002, Review of Educational Research, 72(4), 549-576Obama, Barack The Audacity Of Hope, Vintage Book.

Pellegrino James W., Chudowsky Naomi, and Glaser Robert, Knowing what Students Know, Copyright 2001

The Obama Education Plan, Copyright 2009, Published by Jossey-Bass.

www.bearcent.berkeley.edu

www.nofas.org

www.wcpss.net

http://www.youtube.com/watch?v=X9ap3Iim

Chapter 1.Introdection

The Individuals with Disabilities Education Improvement Act (IDEA) of 2006 and the No

Child Left Behind Act (U.S. Department of Education, 2001) legislation mandate that students

with disabilities be taught to the same high standards as students without disabilities.

What is Fetal Alcohol Syndrome/Effect? According to NOFAS (National Organization on Fetal

Alcohol Syndrome, 1994) that FAS is a series of severe and irreversible physical and mental

birth defects that can include mental retardation, growth deficiencies, craniofacial abnormalities,

central nervous system dysfunction and behavioral maladjustments. Children with Fetal Alcohol

Effects (FAE) exhibit some but not all of the same symptoms. Both FAS and FAE are associated

with lifelong deficiencies in adaptive living skills. The inability to predict consequences,

understand social cues or use appropriate judgment in daily life makes it difficult for those

affected to achieve favorable outcomes in the classroom or to live independently as adults.

FAS/FAE is 100% preventable when a woman abstains from drinking during pregnancy. While

the dangers of maternal alcohol consumption during pregnancy are well documented, the pateral

effects of alcohol on offspring are still large unknown. Vincient A.Spears'older adoptive

daughter has FAE from her biology mother. She used e-toys and other technologies to learn

math, reading and writing.

Transition Planning

1. Define the term "planning" using a source other than our textbook. A) Scheme of

   action or arrangement (American Dictionary 1983), B) Make an arrangement

   for the future (Webster's New English Language Dictionary,2004). C)

Transition Planning: Steps taken by adults to ensure that major periods during a child's early childhood years go smoothly (Transition Planning- Research Starters Education, 2008).

2.   Using that same source, give the source's critical elements of planning. A). Developmentally appropriate education is the first element applies to a number of areas in which young children should be encouraged to grow: cognitive and motor function, attention span and focus, social skills and cooperative play, interest in things outside their immediate environment. Between early childhood and elementary school, a child's mind grows by exploring and discovering it world and through interacting with peers and adults. Teaching at this time should encourage natural curiosity and a love of learning and offer experiences that expand on earlier experiences. Rather than design activates around play or academic subjects, educators should craft lessons that build language, math, and reasoning skills through exploration and cooperative problem solving; B). Parental involvement is another element that is lacking in some program is parental involvement. Parent should not be seen only at drop-off and pick-up times. Successful schools and programs keep an open line of communication between parents and teachers and encourage classroom observation volunteerism, and involvement in policy making. Family diversity should also be embraced, with teachers and administrator welcoming not only parent from different cultures, but also single, teenage, and remarried parents; and C). Support services is the final element that schools and programs have further to go in providing services to children from disadvantage families in

need of child care support, health care services and in case of immigrant families, language support. Boistered in recent years by increased Federal funding and initiative public education is working more than ever with social service agencies, community-based groups, and health care providers to provide comprensive family services and must continue on this trajectory. Support services that strengthen bonds between families and school do more than ensure smooth transitioning and eventual academic success. They build strong, unifies communities (Lombardi, 1992).

3.   According to the information in our text, was anything left out? If so, which element(s)? Be specific. No, Comprehensiveness is same as Developmentally appropriate education; Collaboration and Commitment are the as Parents involvement and Continuity is the same as Support services.

Individual assessments in Speech/Language, Occupational Therapy, and cognitive functioning are necessary in establishing a child's strengths and deficits. Other evaluations which may be helpful are: Psychiatric, neurological and physical therapy.

The child's educational plan should be developed based on the child's individual needs. General educational issues in FAS/FAE children include: hyperactivity(ADDHD),impulsivity,distractibility,poor social skills, poor memory, poor ego developmental, sensory processing dysfunction, sensory defensiveness, scattered cognitive skills, high levels of anxiety and arousal, and learning disabilities. According to the National Research Council (2001); Information technologies are helping to remove some the constraints that have limited assessment practice in the past. Assessment tasks no longer need be confined to paper and pencil formats, and the entire burden of classroom assessment no longer need fall on teacher.

Computer programs that can automatically generate assessment items offer some intriguing possibilities for circumventing this problem and improving the linkage between cognitive theory and observation. The programs are based on a set of item specifications derived from models of the knowledge structures and processes associated with specific characteristics of an item form. For example, the Mathematics Test Creation Assistant has been programmed with specifications for different classes of mathematics problem types for which theory and data exist on the processes involved (Bennett1999).

Environmental needs consist of a low-key or soft room color, low lighting (non-florescent), comfortable temperature, structure, space for movement activities, visual organization, calm area, sensory area.

Program/Curriculum needs should address a balance of child/teacher directed activities, hands-on learning, small class size, flexibility of scheduling, few transitions, consistent adults, integrated teaching, realistic expectations, multi-sensory learning, focus on sensory and ego development and functional social and life skills, rather than academics.According to the web:www.prehall.com/specialed,Children with disabilities in particular need special instructional interventions. FAS/FAE children have opportunity to learn when they have a construct program and activities.Assistive technologies can be classified as low technology, medium technology or high technology. Low technology does use electricty; that is, it neither plugs in nor required a battery. For example, a chess game that is use to teach math. Medium technology uses electricty.For example, PDA, and cell phone. High technology uses computer and e-book (www.prenhall.com/specialed).

Diverse learners or FAS/FAE students use newspapers, periodicals Dora's dolls and software, DVD, or archived document to explore topic bong or in addition to that covered by other students or memory games. They can also use the internet to search for current information or engage in a live "chat" with the author of a book that they read in class (www.prenhall.com/specialed).At the Technolgy for Education website (www.http://tfenc.com), teachers and parents can search by category, vendor, or product name for hundreds of assistive tools. SPAN (Student Parent Access Network) is use help parents with their progress and to learn about computer and networking (www.wcpss.net).

This learner travel through the pages of this article "Stand by me", the learner began to wonder how do teachers cope with the pressures of teaching? Standards, testing and accountability is latest venue where, according to teachers, too many student ratio to teachers in the classrooms and not enough support. The teachers believe in higher standard but do not believe in standardize test playing the great part, it playing now. Where students and teachers spent a lot of times preparing for the test like the end of grade test in the state of N.C.; when the students failed the test then the teachers are held accountability (Stand by me p9 and 11). Who should set the standards? A significant number of teachers (42%), for example, have said adjustments are needed in the drive to raise standards, and teachers in focus groups often questioned whether higher academic standards always reflect achievable educational goals. Almost all teachers (93%) say education professionals, not elected officials, should be setting them.

But much of teachers' criticism focuses not the standards themselves, but on testing. Teachers have repeatedly acknowledged that test have benefits: They prompt students to work harder (75%) and identify those who need tutoring or summer school (62%). But most teachers (53%) also say that standardized tests are a "seriously flawed" measure of student learning. Another 24% say tests are important, but there are serious problems with how their district uses them. Less than 1 in 5 (18%) says tests are meaningful and their district uses them well.

A majority of teachers (79%) also believe that testing invariably leads to "teaching to the test," although most (73%) say they do not resort to these themselves. For a majority (61%), teaching to test" inevitably stifles real teaching and learning." About a third (34%) says it is fine as long as the test measures the right things.

Prepared to live with it, still, most teachers seem prepared to live with testing despite their complaints about the ways it is used and could be used in the future. Most (62%) see it as "a necessary evil," agreeing that "ultimately, the schools need some kind of standardized assessment." Almost 1 in 5 teachers (18%) say "standardized tests do much harm than good-the schools would be better off if they were completely abandoned" (Stand by Me, p13).

"Education is what survives when what has been learned has been forgotten" (B.F. Skinner, New Scientist, May 12, 1964). Despite the myriad of obstacles teachers come up against, almost 2 in 3 (65%) say they believe that truly good teachers can overcome societal barriers such as poverty or uninvolved parents and still get their students to learn what they are supported to (Stand By Me, p 16). The movies the "Ron Clark's Story, Lean on Me and Sister Act 2" shown how to reach the students of inner-city schools with music. This learner believes that all teachers can be good teachers, if they get the support from the schools, government and parents. Not all tests are evil but need not to be the only answer to education crisis. Have pre-test at the beginning of the year and have relaxed time in the classrooms.

Chapter 2:   Literature Review and Case Studies.

Literature Review:

Abstract: The BEAR Assessment System (BAS; Wilson Sloan, 2000) is an integrated approach to developing assessments that provide meaningful interpretations of student work relative to the cognitive and developmental goals of a curriculum.

It is grounded by four key principles guiding assessment development and includes four building blocks (Wilson, 2005) that are tools for constructing meaningful assessments aligned with curricular goals and instructional activities. These principles are: 1.Assessment should be based on a developmental perspective of student learning, 2.What is taught and what is assessed must be clearly aligned, 3. Teachers are the managers and users of assessment data and Classroom assessment must uphold sound standards of validity and reliability. The BEAR Assessment System includes four building blocks for constructing quality assessments: 1. Construct Maps, 2. Items Design, 3. The Outcome Space, and 4.The Measurement Model. Cons: Students have a 50-50 chance of responding correctly to map assessment and it is a data driven approach to teaching. This learner is not a MapQuest student as the BEAR Assessment used and it is harder for teachers to learn and get training on the BEAR Assessment. Teachers need to be train in using the BEAR in teaching FAS/E children. Stating from the book the Fantastic Antoine Succeeds (Kleinfeld, J. and Westcott, S., 1993), Individual assessment in Speech/Language, Occupational Therapy, and cognitive functioning are necessary in establishing a child's strengths and deficits. Other evaluations which may be helpful are: Psychiatric, neurological and physical therapy. The child's educational plan should be developed based on the child's individual needs.

Abstract: The Case OF Parental Involvement Programs:

The authors (Mattingly, D.J., Prislin, R., Mckenzie, T.L., Rodriquez, and J.L., and Kayzar, B. 2002, Review of Educational Research, 72(4), 549-576.) analyzed 41 studies that evaluated K-12 parental involvement programs in order to assess claims that such programs are an effective means of improving student learning. The authors found that the majority of existing evidence regarding the links between parental involvement and student achievement comes from correlation studies rather than rigorous, systematic evaluations of the impact programs have on student learning(p.550).Of the 41 studies, the authors found only four that used the most rigorous research design. The authors also noted that majority of intervention programs they reviewed focused on changing parent behavior especially in the areas of parenting and supporting home learning –rather than on changing teacher practices or school structures.

Abstract: Proven Ideas from Research for Parents.

This booklet (Armbruster, B., Lehr, F., Osborn, J.B. 2003, A Child Becomes A Reader K-3, Second Edition.) contains a short summary of what scientific research says about how children learn to read and write; things that parents and other caregivers can do to enable a child to become a successful reader and writer at three different grade levels; a list of helpful terms; and ideas for books and organizations that may be of interest to parents and other caregivers.

Affect Of Title I Parental Involvement on Student Reading and Mathematics Achievement.

This quasi-experimental (Shaver, A.V., and Walls, R.T. 1998, Journal of Research and Development in Education, 31(2), 90-97.) study examines the effects of parental involvement on the reading and math achievement of 335 Title I students in second through eighth grades, and their parents. The students who participated in the study all were receiving remedial help in reading and math. Information about their achievement levels was based on pre- and post-test on the Comprehensive Test of Basic Skills (CTBS/4) in reading and math. The district developed a series of three-hour parent workshops that involved information, training, and discussions. The researchers found that students whose parents regularly attended school-based parent workshops made greater gains in reading and math than students with less-involved parents. From tne book Fantastic Antone Succeeds (Kleinfeld, J., and Westcott, S., 1993, p.141), Since children with FAS/FAE often learn better when they gain information from as many senses as possible, parents need to provide learning opportunities in as many modalities as possible. Alcohol-affected children who do not get home support or who come to us very late look very different from those who have experienced the benefits of early intervention. When we see these children, they tend to be six to twelve months behind in developmental delevelopmental level at age three. Early intervention cannot overcome the damage of alcohol. But early intervention can dramatically improve the child's life skills and can lay the foundation for later development (p.147).

Conclusion:

As it includes a review of scientific research on parental and family influences on children's development of language and early reading skills. When parent's takes interest in their children's reading, the students are able to master many tasks in education (President Obama and Dr. Bill Crosby, 2009). According to NOFAS (www.nofas.org)"What is the optimum school room environment for students with FAS/FAE?Children with FAS/FAE function best with there is structure, order, and routine. Too often, they are punished, teased, humiliated,or rejected because they cannot "keep up "with their classmates. The reality is that they have a birth defect that causes them to think, act, and relate differently than other students. Once in school, they need and deserve to learn as much as they are capable of in a safe, healthy, caring environment. While we know that children with FAS/FAE function best in small classrooms with one-to-one on supervision, such ideal conditions are unlikely to be found in the many schools working with limited resources and facing even more budget cuts.

References:

Addison, J.T. (1992). Urie Bronfenbrenner. Human Ecology, 20(2), 16-20.

Armbruster, B., Lehr, F., Osborn, J.B. 2003, A Child Becomes A Reader K-3, Second Edition

BAS; Wilson&Sloan, 2000) "

Desimone, L., Finn-Stevenson, M., and Henrich, C. (200) Whole School Reform In A Low-Income African American Community: The Effects Of The CoZi Model On Teachers, Parents, And Students. Urban Education, 35 (3), 269-323.

Stephen Crowley/The New York Times

President Obama spoke about changes in the No Child Left Behind law Friday during a ceremony at the White House.

By SAM DILLON

Published: September 23, 2011

With his declaration on Friday that he would waive the most contentious provisions of a federal education law, President Obama effectively rerouted the nation's education history after a turbulent decade of overwhelming federal influence.

Related

Times Topic: No Child Left Behind Act

Mr. Obama invited states to reclaim the power to design their own school accountability and improvement systems, upending the centerpiece of the Bush-era No Child Left Behind law, a requirement that all students be proficient in math and reading by 2014.

"This does not mean that states will be able to lower their standards or escape accountability," the president said. "If states want more flexibility, they're going to have to set higher standards, more honest standards that prove they're serious about meeting them."

But experts said it was a measure of how profoundly the law had reshaped America's public school culture that even in states that accept the administration's offer to pursue a new agenda, the law's legacy will live on in classrooms, where educators' work will continue to emphasize its major themes, like narrowing student achievement gaps, and its tactics, like using standardized tests to measure educators' performance.

In a White House speech, Mr. Obama said states that adopted new higher standards, pledged to overhaul their lowest-performing schools and revamped their teacher evaluation systems should apply for waivers of 10 central provisions of the No Child law, including its 2014 proficiency deadline. The administration was forced to act, Mr. Obama said, because partisan gridlock kept Congress from updating the law.

"Given that Congress cannot act, I am acting," Mr. Obama said. "Starting today, we'll be giving states more flexibility."

But while the law itself clearly empowers Secretary of Education Arne Duncan to waive its provisions, the administration's decision to make the waivers conditional on states' pledges to pursue Mr. Obama's broad school improvement agenda has angered Republicans gearing up for the 2012 elections.

On Friday Congressional leaders immediately began characterizing the waivers as a new administration power grab, in line with their portrayal of the health care overhaul, financial sector regulation and other administration initiatives.

"In my judgment, he is exercising an authority and power he doesn't have," said Representative John Kline, Republican of Minnesota and chairman of the House education committee. "We all know the law is broken and needs to be changed. But this is part and parcel with the whole picture with this administration: they cannot get their agenda through Congress, so they're doing it with executive orders and rewriting rules. This is executive overreach."

Mr. Obama made his statements to a bipartisan audience that included Gov. Bill Haslam of Tennessee, a Republican, Gov. Lincoln Chafee of Rhode Island, an independent, and 24 state superintendents of education.

"I believe this will be a transformative movement in American public education," Christopher Cerf, New Jersey's education commissioner under Gov. Chris Christie, a Republican, said after the speech.

The No Child law that President George W. Bush signed in 2002 was a bipartisan rewrite of the basic federal law on public schools, first passed in 1965 to help the nation's neediest students. The 2002 law required all schools to administer reading and math tests every year, and to increase the proportion of students passing them until reaching 100 percent in 2014. Schools that failed to keep pace were to be labeled as failing, and eventually their principals fired and staffs dismantled. That system for holding schools accountable for test scores has encouraged states to lower standards, teachers to focus on test preparation, and math and reading to crowd out history, art and foreign languages.

Mr. Obama's blueprint for rewriting the law, which Congress has never acted on, urged lawmakers to adopt an approach that would encourage states to raise standards, focus interventions only on the worst failing schools and use test scores and other measures to evaluate teachers' effectiveness. In its current proposal, the administration requires states to adopt those elements of its blueprint in exchange for relief from the No Child law.

Mr. Duncan, speaking after Mr. Obama's speech, said the waivers could bring significant change to states that apply. "For parents, it means their schools won't be labeled failures," Mr. Duncan said. "It should reduce the pressure to teach to the test."

Critics were skeptical, saying that classroom teachers who complain about unrelenting pressure to prepare for standardized tests were unlikely to feel much relief.

"In the system that N.C.L.B. created, standardized tests are the measure of all that is good, and that has not changed," said Monty Neill, executive director of Fair Test, an antitesting advocacy group. "This policy encourages states to use test scores as a significant factor in evaluating teachers, and that will add to the pressure on teachers to teach to the test."

Randi Weingarten, president of the American Federation of Teachers, said her union favored evaluation systems that would help teachers improve their instruction, whereas the administration was focusing on accountability. "You're seeing an extraordinary change of policy, from an accountability system focused on districts and schools, to accountability based on teacher and principal evaluations," Ms. Weingarten said.

For most states, obtaining a waiver could be the easy part of accepting the administration's invitation. Actually designing a new school accountability system, and obtaining statewide acceptance of it, represents a complex administrative and political challenge for governors and other state leaders, said Gene Wilhoit, executive director of the Council of Chief State School Officers, which the White House said played an important role in developing the waiver proposal.

Only about five states may be ready to apply immediately, and perhaps 20 others could follow by next spring, Mr. Wilhoit said. Developing new educator evaluation systems and other aspects of follow-through could take states three years or more, he said.

Officials in New York, New Jersey and Connecticut, and in at least eight other states — Colorado, Florida, Georgia, Kentucky, Idaho, Minnesota, Virginia and Wisconsin — said Friday that they would probably seek the waivers.

Abstract: Major national surveys of public school teachers over the last decade exploring topics ranging from curriculum to parents to standards and testing. In fact, we briefly revisit the standards and testing issue here to gauge teachers' reactions to changes taking place under the No Child Left behind Act of 2001, which mandates annual testing for students and sets out explicit consequences for schools where students repeatedly fail. Exploring teachers' views and getting their counsel on what would improve education and help them to better do their jobs is a matter of wide interest. After all, teachers are the ones doing the doing. Their views should be taken very seriously ("Stand By Me "p9).

The teachers believe in higher standard but do not believe in standardize test playing the great part, it playing now. Where students and teachers spent a lot of times preparing for the test like the end of grade test in the state of N.C.; when the students failed the test then the teachers are held accountability (Stand by Me p9 and 11). Who should set the standards? A significant number of teachers (42%), for example, have said adjustments are needed in the drive to raise standards, and teachers in focus groups often questioned whether higher academic standards always reflect achievable educational goals. Almost all teachers (93%) say education professionals, not elected officials, should be setting them.

But much of teachers' criticism focuses not the standards themselves, but on testingfor challenging children, like Fetal Alcohol Syndrome/Fetal Alcohol Effect. Teachers have repeatedly acknowledged that test have benefits: They prompt students to work harder (75%) and identify those who need tutoring or summer school (62%). But most teachers (53%) also say that standardized tests are a "seriously flawed" measure of student learning. Another 24% say tests are important, but there are serious problems with how their district uses them. Less than 1 in 5 (18%) says tests are meaningful and their district uses them well.

A majority of teachers (79%) also believe that testing invariably leads to "teaching to the test," although most (73%) say they do not resort to these themselves. For a majority (61%), teaching to test" inevitably stifles real teaching and learning." About a third (34%) says it is fine as long as the test measures the right things.

Almost 1 in 5 teachers (18%) say "standardized tests do much harm than good-the schools would be better off if they were completely abandoned" (Stand By Me, p13).

"Education is what survives when what has been learned has been forgotten" (B.F. Skinner, New Scientist, May 12, 1964). Despite the myriad of obstacles teachers come up against, almost 2 in 3 (65%) say they believe that truly good teachers can overcome societal barriers such as poverty or uninvolved parents and still get their students to learn what they are supported to (Stand By Me, p 16). The movies the "Ron Clark's Story, Lean On Me and Sister Act 2" shown how to reach the students of inner-city schools with music. This learner believes that all teachers can be good teachers, if they get the support from the schools, government and parents. Not all tests are evil but need not to be the only answer to education crisis.

Abstract: The Essential 55 is book and article by Ron Clark that brings out the best in students by using tools to help them learn. It created respect for students and teachers by using theory of "You are ok and I am ok, and the Golden Rule: Do unto other as you would have them do unto you "(**www.ask.com,p1**).

Some of the Essential 55 showed me how to teach in my home with mundane nature. For example, "If you don't say thank you within 30 seconds, I'm taking it back." Or, "If someone asks you a question, you need to answer it and then ask a question yourself."

Here are some of the ideas that Ron Clark says are essential for kids to learn:

1. Make eye contact.

2. Respect other; ideas and opinions.

3. Do not save seats.

4. Say thank you within three seconds of receiving something.

5. When you win, do not brag; when you lose, do not show anger.

6. Do your homework each and every night without fail.

7. Be the best person you can be.

8. Always be honest.

9. If you are asked a question in conversation, ask a question in return.

10. Stand up for what you believe in (Beth Lewis, www.about.com, p1).

Teachers are concerned about disrespectful, unruly, rude students in the focus groups for Stand By Me article and the movies: Ron Clark's Story, Sister Act 2 and Lean On Me, students walk around through the halls, in the classrooms and cursing and do whatever they want (Stand By Me, p16). This learner learned from Ron Clark's article and book that you can not assessing students, if they are not under control and if they do not respect themselves and others. Teaching Fetal Alcohol Syndrome/Effect children to respect each other is halp the battle for them to learn.

Southwest Educational Development Laboratory.(2003) Compendium of Research Based Resources for Parental Involvement. Diversity and School, Family, and Community Connections. Austin, Texas

This synthesis reviews research finding from 64 studies that address some aspect of diversity as it relates to student achievement and school, family, and community connections. It describes the procedures used to select the studies and a brief overview of the board concepts related to diversity and family involvement that the studies address. This review examines the growing evidence that family and community connections with schools make a difference in student success(Henderson, Anne T., and Mapp, Karen 2002).The authors look at 51 recent studies-all but two published between 1995 and 2002,covering a range of perspective and approaches. The studies some of which are based on scientific research, fall in three broad categories:1)studies on the impact of family and community involvement on student achievement;2)studies on effective strategies to connect schools, family, and communities; and 3) studies on parent and community organizing efforts to improve schools.

Effect of Title I Parental Involvement on Student Reading and Mathematics Achievement. This quasi-experimental (Shaver, A.V., and Walls, R.T. 1998, Journal of Research and Development in Education, 31(2), 90-97.) study examines the effects of parental involvement on the reading and math achievement of 335 Title I students in second through eighth grades, and their parents. The students who participated in the study all were receiving remedial help in reading and math. Information about their achievement levels was based on pre- and post-test on the Comprehensive Test of Basic Skills (CTBS/4) in reading and math. The district developed a series of three-hours parent workshops that involved information, training, and discussions. The researchers found that students whose parents regularly attended school-based parent workshops made greater gains in reading and math than students with less-involved parents.

References:

Addison, J.T. (1992). Urie Bronfenbrenner. Human Ecology, 20(2), 16-20.

Armbruster, B., Lehr, F., Osborn, J.B. 2003, A Child Becomes A Reader K-3, Second Edition

BAS; Wilson Sloan, 2000)

Clark Ron (2003), The Essential 55, Hyperion Publish, New York, NY

Clark Ron (2004), The Excellent 11, Hyperion Publish, New York, NY.

Desimone, L., Finn-Stevenson, M., and Henrich, C. (200) Whole School Reform In A Low-Income African American Community: The Effects Of The CoZi Model On Teachers, Parents, And Students. Urban Education, 35 (3), 269-323.

Kleinfeld, Judith, and Wescott, Siobhan. Fantastic Antone Succeeds! University of Alaska Press.1993

Mattingly, D.J., Prislin, R., Mckenzie, T.L., Rodriquez, and J.L., and Kayzar, B. 2002, Review of Educational Research, 72(4), 549-576Obama, Barack The Audacity Of Hope, Vintage Book.

Pellegrino James W., Chudowsky Naomi, and Glaser Robert, Knowing what Students Know, Copyright 2001

The Obama Education Plan, (Copyright 2009), Published by Jossey-Bass.

Wadsworth Deborah (2002) Article "Stand By Me"

www.bearcent.berkeley.edu /10/20/2008

www.nofas.org /08/24/2008

www.wcpss.net/11/20/2010

http://www.youtube.com/watch?v=X9ap3Iimim

Michael's school issues that he is facing.

Reform No Child Left Behind Law: Obama and Biden will reform NCLB, which starts by funding the law. Obama and Biden believe teachers should not be forced to spend the academic year preparing students to fill in bubbles on standardized test (The Obama Education Plan, Copyright, 2009). If Michael can not stay awake then he will fail the test and he will be left behind. Address the Dropout Crisis; Obama and Biden will address the dropout crisis by passing legislation to provide funding to school districts to invest in intervention (The Obama Education Plan, Copyright, 2009).If Michael got to work a full-time job to supported his family then he would have to dropout of school. Obama and Biden will work to ensure the academic success of students with disabilities by increasing funding and effectively enforcing the Individuals with Disabilities Education Act, and by holding schools accountable for providing students with disabilities the services and supports they need to reach their potential (The Obama Education Plan, Copyright, 2009). Michael's stress and worrying about completing school, may cause him into depression with is a mental disability disorder. According to the textbook: Instructional Technology and Media for Learning, Ninth Edition (Smaldino, Sharon E., Lowther, Deborah l., Russell, James D.,Copyright,2008), A growing number of virtual high schools, schools using the Internet for delivery, offer courses or whole programs of study (Wood, 2005). Students can access courses that might not be available to them at their local schools. Students can take advanced placement classes from other high schools or from colleges and universities anywhere in the world. It is possible to obtain a high school or college diploma without ever having set foot in a classroom. There are many software applications (WebCT, Blackboard) that provide both ease of access to the instruction and resources for the instructor and students for successful study online. There are issues that need to be addressed by anyone wishing to venture into this area of academic study:

1. Credential of the institution offering the degree.

2. Quality and rigor of the courses.

3. Cost associated with online courses, such as the equipment requirements, online charges, and tuition.

References:

Smaldino, Sharon E., Lowther, Deborah L., Russell, James D., Instructional Technology and Media for Learning, Ninth Edition, Copyright, 2008

The Obama Education Plan, Copyright, 2009.

www.cyberbee.com/

www.classroom.net

www.cnn.comwww.wcpss.net/SPAN

Case Study II Technology for all schools.

According to Warschauer (2005/2006) ,Casey attended Mountain Springs High School, which is a large school mainly made up of students of the upper class status, while John attended Friendly High School, a small rural school mainly composed of students lower to middle class status.

Casey is candidate for a college scholarship and he has many opportunities at Mountain Springs High School for technology scholarships, like John who attends smaller school that does has opportunity for technology scholarships. When Casey enrolled in the school in the ninth grade, each student was issued a laptop computer to use for remainder of his or her high school career. This was helpful to Casey in that it allows him to used software for writing, research, appling for scholarships and science projects. But, John enrolled in the ninth grade at Friendly High School, there was rarely time to use computer because there was one computer per grade level and one lab that has 20 highly used computers. John's teacher is very technology and computer savvy and loves to learn and teach technology and computer. John 's classroom contains least 30 students that must shared the computer and computer lab but John could goes to the library for study hall and use the computer there and on weekend,John could goes to the public library to use the computer. John could ask his teacher to help him with his work. John is a smart student whom planed to attend college but he knows that his parents can not afford it. But, he can apply for grant, community scholarship and Gates Foundation Scholarship. John is jealous of Casey because of the technology and computer advantage at his school (Warschauer, Mark 2005/2006). According to court case Williams v. California (2004), which addressed the issue of educational quality that affected educational outcomes of poor students. Two basic issues were presented in this case: First, does the state of California provide all students the basic resources needed to learn such as qualified teachers, sufficient instructional materials, and adequate facilities? And second, should all students have a fundamental right to an equal education?

Williams, the plaintiff, argued that California's public education failed on both issues by not providing students the necessary educational resources, leading to unequal results across the schools in the state. Brown v.Board of Education was about separate but no equal, CFE v. State of New York was about accountability& funding reforms and Montoy v.State of Kansas, involving educational adequacy& state's school finance plan violates the state constitution [Essex, Nathan L.,(2008, 2005, 2002, 1999), School Law and the Public Schools, Fourth Edition, p.363.].

References:

Essex, Nathan L.,(2008, 2005, 2002, 1999), School Law and the Public Schools, Fourth Edition, p.363.

Warschaue Mark (2005/2006) Going one to one, Educational leadership p.34-38

Yudof Mark G., Kirp David L., Levin Betsy, Moran Rachel F.,(2002), Educational Policy and the Law, Fourth Edition, p.767.

http://www.edu/edtechcases

Introduction: These articles are about technologies for Disabilities students and how technologies are use to teach Disabilities students.

Smartpen technology use to help blind college students with subjects like biology, calculus and physics. Smartpen and Paper technology work with touch and records classroom audio aims to bring these subjects to life for blind students (Science Daily, Dec.11, 2007)."Mainstream approaches to teaching STEM (science, technology, engineering and math) course all rely strongly on diagrams, graphs, charts and other figures, putting students with visual disabilities at a significant disadvantage, "Andy Van Schaack, lecturer in Vanderbilt University's Peabody College of education and human development, said", Our goal is to enable students and teachers to produce and explore diagrams and figures through touch and sound using a smartpen and paper technology that is low-cost, Portable and easy to use"(Science Daily,Dec.11,2007). According to Van Schaack and colleague Joshua Mele, a research at Smith-Kettlewell Eye Research Institute who is blind, have received a $300, 00.00 grant from the National Science Foundation to new technology, created by technology company Livescribe, to effort Van Schaack is Liverscribe's senior science adviser.

Van Schaach area of expertise is instructional technology. He spend a lot of his time trying to figure out how to use technology to make teaching and learning more effective, efficient and accessible, Van Schaack said "A new world of possibilities has opened for the rapid creation of portable, low-cost, high-quality accessible graphics enhanced with audio. For example, a visually impaired psychology student could learn neuroanatomy by exploring a diagram of the brain with each lobe, gyrus and suicus's name spoken as the smartpen touches it" (Science Daily, Dec.11, 2007).

Smartpen recognizes handwritten marks through a camera inside its tip that focuses on a minute pattern of dots(like Braille system, http://duxburysystems.com/downloads/duxbrif.exe) printed on paper, it captures over 100 hours of audio through a built-in microphone and plays audio back through a build-in speaker or 3D recording headset. Files are uploaded from to a computer using a USB connection. The technology will be much more affordable and portable than previous products used for this purpose; students can just put it in their backpacks with the rest of their books and notebooks (Science Daily, Dec.11, 2007). The Smartpen is in store now at the cost of $200.00 or less. Livescribe interactive notebooks cost about the same. This technology is affordable for the students at Governor Morehead School for the blind in Raleigh, N.C.

"New Teaching Tools Aid Visually Impaired Students in Learning Math" (Science Daily, April 16, 2010).

Mathematics can be challenging for many students but researchers have found that children with Visual Impairments face disproportionate challenges learning math and by the time they reach the college level, they are significantly, mathematics and engineering disciplines. At the University of Illinois are helping shapes the futures of children with visual disabilities by creating innovative teaching tools that are expected to help the children learn mathematics more easily and perhaps multifly their career opportunities when they reach adulthood (Science Daily, April 16,2010). About 5 million or 1 out 20 preschool age children and about 12.1 million children ages 6-17 have visual impairments, according to the Braille Institute (Science Daily, April 16, 2010). Shella Schneider, who is a senior and the first student who is legally blind to major in sculpture in the School of Art Design within the College of Fine and Applied Arts at Illinois, is creating a series of small sculpture with mathematical equations imprinted on them in Braille that will be use to help children with visual impairments learn mathematics. The equations will be written in Nemeth Code, a form of Braille used for mathematical and scientific symbols (Science Daily, April 16, 2010). Deana McDonagh stated "The sculptures are organic forms that are designed to be hand-held by children around the ages of 7-10" (Professor of industrial design at University of Illinois).Professor McDonagh designed project through the viewpoint of a younger child. When the students played with fun educational tools then run their hand over them, they will realize that there is Braille equations embedded within the forms (Science Daily, April 16, 2010). According to Schneider, that traditionally children with visual disabilities are taught to solve mathematical problems using abacuses, a tool that may seem antiquated in today's world.

" We're trying to bring the education of visually impaired children more up to date, rather than relying on staid methods of doing things", Schneider said. "We're hoping to eliminate this idea that blind children have to write math with an abacus because they can't see to write on a piece of paper (Science Daily, April 16, 2010).

Schneider sculpted six models each a few inches in diameter, from cubes of balsa foam. The models are being translated into three-dimensional computer images to finalize the shapes and position the equations before the sculptures are cast from handing and occasionally being dropped (Science Daily, April 16, 2010). Braille system use 6 dots system.

"Where you and I might place the Braille equations are of no consequence," McDonagh said "When children with visual impairments are handing the sculptures, and reading them with their fingertips, it's got to make sense to them place the Braille in three-dimensional space" (Science Daily, April 16, 2010).

"Virtual Reality teaches Autistic Children "and Autistic children learn from "Virtual Peers" (Science Daily, March 5, 2008).

University of Haifa found that children with autism improved their road safety skills after practicing with a unique Virtual Reality System." Children with autism rarely have opportunities to experience or to learn to cope with day-to-day situation. Using Virtual simulations such as the one used in research enables them to acquire skills that will make it possible for them to become independent", said Professors Josman and Weiss, from the Department of Occupational Therapy at the University of Haifa (Science Daily, Jan. 29, 2008). According to Professors' Josman and Weiss, six autistic students ages 7-12 spent one month learning how to cross virtual street to wait for the virtual light at the left and right for virtual cars using a simulation programmed by Yuval Naveh (Science Daily, Jan. 29, 2008). The best way to teach children with autism skills is through repeated practice in natural settings, but the danger of learning to cross the street in a natural setting obviously prohibits this method. This is where virtual reality is very effective, as demonstrated by the research team (University of Haifa, Science Daily, and Jan. 29, 2008) which included Hadass Milika Ben-Cham, then a student in the Occupational Therapy master's program and Shula Friedrich, the principal of the Haifa Ofer School for Children with Autism as well as Professors Josman and Weiss. According to Yuval Naveh, children in the study showed substantial improvement throughout the learning process: at the beginning of the study, the average child was able to use the 2nd level of the software while by the end they mastered the 9th level, which is characterized by more vehicles traveling at a higher speed. Northwestern University researchers use virtual peers to teach children with Autism in school and home." Children with high-functioning autism may be able to give you a lecture on a topic of great interest to them but they can't carry contingent or two-way conversation," stated by Professor Justine Cassell (Director of Northwestern's Center for Technology and Social Behavior). Professor Cassell and researcher Andrea Tartaro collected data from six children with high-functioning autism aged 7 to 11 as they engaged in play during an hour-long session with a real-child, and with a virtual peer name Sam (Science Daily, Jan. 29, 2008).Virtual Reality and Virtual Peers reach Autistic children where other education programs could not.

"Virtual Lab "by University of Virginia

According to University of Virginia students learning science in the classroom can now give their textbooks a break, and learn basic science concepts online. The virtual lab, developed by engineers to guides students through 50 experiments, along with text and vivid animations that explain how things work (Science Daily, Aug.1, 2007). The University of Virginia's virtual lab helps students look inside the things we use every day to see how they work. The system uses emerging software visualization tools to explain common technologies; there are currently eight virtual labs on the website: electronics, a microelectronics teaching lab. "The thing about virtual reality is I can show thing that are invisible. One of the things that we depict frequently is electrical fields. You can't see those. I can make them visible with virtual reality," said John Bean, an engineer at the University of Virginia. The Virtual Lab is brainchild of electrical engineer professor John Bean, who wanted to find a way for kids to able to take apart a device to see how it work, them put it back together again. Consulting with two high school science teachers, he learned that student loved in-class demonstrations to illustrate basic concepts like change attraction and repulsion. But while entertaining, the instructors found it difficult to explain the science behind the demonstrations and illustrate it visually Professor Bean (Aug. 1, 2007).

The term "virtual reality" is often used to describe interactive software programs in which the user responds to visual and hearing cues as he or she navigates a 3D environment on graphics monitor. But originally, it referred to total virtual environment, in which the user would be immersed in an artificial, three-dimensional computer-generated world, involving not just sight and sound, but touch as well. Devices that simulate touch experience are called haptic devices. Computer modeling is used to simulate the structure and appearance of both static objects, such as building architecture, and dynamic situations, such as a football game. Computer modeling can enable the user to test the consequences of choices and decisions. They can provide cutaway views that let you see aspects, as well as visualization tools that can provide many different perspectives. Physical models that reproduce behavior are limited by the physics of the world, while computer models have much looser bounds. Computer models enable you to run companies and civilizations, fight battles, play football games and evolve new species (Aug. 1, 2007).Technologies take many forms and functions that can teach other. But it must be affordable and an access to all.

Summary;

These articles are about teaching disabilities student with technologies like virtual world, games, labs and smartpen. Disabilities students use Alternative keyboards such as Intellitools'IntelliKeys, voice recognition software such as Dragon Talk's Dragon Naturally Speaking. The blind students use smartpen and JAWS for Windows and optical character recognition software. Innovative advances in technology assist teachers to better meet the special needs of students with learning or physical disabilities, as well gifted students. Technologies are use for Individualized Education Programs for special needs learners and by integrating assistive technology into classroom instructional practices (www.iowa-iep.net). These technologies help support the No Child Left Behind Act.

References:

Roblyer M.D & Doering Aaron H., (2010, 2006, 2003, 2000, 1997) Integrating Educational Technology Teaching, Fifth Edition, p.414

Smaldino Sharon E., Lowther Deborah L & Russell James D., (2008, 2005, 2002, 1999, 1996) Instructional Technology and Media for Learning, p.338

http://www.sciencedaily.com

Technology and computer cannot replace teachers.

Can computers effectively replace teachers? Take a stand, one way or the other, and clearly indicate your choice.

No, Remind me of Commander DATA of the New Generation, Star Trek; He is a man-like robot who want to be human and irobot in the movie "irobot" has a human implant in his CP that's able him to act like human but the are not human. Computers and new technologies cannot tihink, feel or react to human students needs. The relationships a child develops in school become critical to his or her positive development. Because of the amount of time children spend in school, the relationships fostered there carry real weight (Family American.com, 1990). Also children may for the first time be developing relationships with adult outside their home and family. These connection help a child develop cognitively and emotionally (www.bronfenbrenner.com). Computer does not teach that or feel that. Computers and technologies are tools that can help one to learn in formations. The term" learning styles" is commonly use throughout various educational fields and therefore, has many connotations. In general, it refers to the uniqueness of how each learner receives and processes new information through their senses. The National Association of Secondary School Principals defines learning style as." the compost site of characteristic cognitive, affective, and physiological factors that serve as relatively stable indicators of how a learner perceives intacts with, and responds to the learning environment"(www.vark-learning.com).

According to Neil Postman, chairman of the Department of Culture and Communications at New York University, calls the "god of Technology" in his essay(April,2001) "Virtual Students Digital Classroom". The explosive growth of computer technology and the internet over the past decade has deluded many Americans into believing that technology is the answer to most if not all of our problems. It is the Information Age, they say, and once we have enough information at our disposal, we'll be able to make the world a better place.

Computer can check a paper's spelling and grammar, but they cannot teach someone style or help clarify an idea. They can give a grade, but cannot pat someone on the back. They can display a novel chapter or poem to the screen, but cannot sit in middle of a group of children and read it with the right voies.They can display a three-dimensional model of a sodium chloride molecule, but cannot answer a question about it unless the programmers who designed the model had anticipated the question beforehand. They can tell the story of the Alamo, complete with pictures and sounds, but cannot tell what it feels like to walk inside the room where Jim Bowie died. They can tell a student that his or her answer is wrong, but cannot wipe away the frustrated tear that may follow. They can record whether a student is present is present in class, but cannot ask why the student looks nervous or angry or depressed. They can print a story that student has written, but cannot recognize its potential and encourage the student to keep writing (http://www.andybox.com/?page_id=75).Computers and technologies can teach about the Civil Right Movement, but cannot feel the joy of Afro-American when Sen.Barack Obama was elected president of the USA.

References:

Campbell, L., & Campbell, B. (1992). Teaching and learning through Multiple

Intelligences. Seattle, WA: New Horizons for Learning.

Postman, N., (April 2001) Virtual Students, Digital Classroom.

http://www.andybox.com/?page_id=75).

www.bronfenbrenner.com

www.Family American.com, 1990

Distance Learning

According to textbook: Educational leadership and Planning for Technology (Picciano, Anthony G.2006) ; Distance education is the term that has most commonly been used for several decades. A term for the physical separation of teachers and learners, where learners take on greater responsibility for their learning, as is frequently the case when doing so from a distance. Asynchronous: Happening at different times, communication is characterized by time-independence; that is, the sender and receiver do not communicate at the same time. An example is electronic mall (Picciano, 2006). Face to Face learning is in the classroom. Synchronous: Happening at the same time, communication is characterized by time-dependence; that is, the sender and receiver communicate at the same time. An example is a telephone conversation (Picciano, 2006).

Vincient A. Spears traveled to distance learning planets. The first planet was In See See You in 1976 to 1980 where he physically attend education program of Criminal Justice (NCCU,1980, BA), then traveled to the planet of US Army (1980 to 1983, Medical Specialist), then traveled to planet of Correspondent Schools: ICS(Basic Computer Programmer) and Kensington University (Law School,2001,JD), where the distance learning was by mail, then planet of online schools (Capella University for only a year and Strayer University, learning on blackboard). Accorded to Dr.Angie Parker (Yavapai College, Distributed Learning), Colleges continue offer growing numbers of courses and programs of study through distance education technologies. At the millennium, the Association of Governing Boards of Universities and Colleges estimated that one-third of all colleges and universities would be closing with ten years.

Accorded to Peter Drucker, a management theorist, recently predicted that higher education institution as we know them today will be relics in a matter of a few short years (Lenzer, 1997).

In addition to the need for change, is the need to work within new budgetary constraints being set forth by legislatures across the nation? These budget cuts are threatening to derail many traditional programs in higher education, forcing colleges and universities to look to faculty for cost saving distance delivery alternatives. Distance delivery has proven to be a means of recouping lost revenue, but without will faculty, the programs are destined for collapse. If distance education is not only to sustain itself but to grow in upcoming years, it is imperative for administrators to understand the motivation that entices faculty to transition to alternative delivery modes. A number of authors have taken on the task of investigating incentives which translate into the distance learning paradigm (Betts, 1998; Rockwell, Schauer, Fritz & Marx, 1999; Wills, 1994; Wilson, 1998). The success of any future distance education program is hanged on enticing faculty to move their courses to distant formats. Flexible scheduling also allows a wider audience of potential learners to access instruction. Technology-mediated instruction can be accessed 24/7 from nearly any location, opening potential for working students, parents of young children, and those with disabilities to reach their educational goals. Moore (2001) relates that the advent of interactive media and flexible scheduling has also brought forth a new generation of distance faculty who are now able to teach while pursuing other interests. Workload was also addressed from the perspective of class size. Class size policies are widely diverse and have a direct tie to the budget. Although numerous studies (Bower, 2001: Mckenzie, Mims, Bennett & Waugh, 2002) present the incentive of smaller class sizes, colleges are reluctant to limit registrations. Faculty, on the other hand, question the quality of instruction with class loads exceeding twenty-five students. raves (2000) suggests that class size policies remain consistent between online and traditional, while Miller (2000) suggests a sliding scale of stipends for faculty who teach courses in excess of twenty-five students. Dillon (1998) and Dillon and Walsh (1998) add to the literature on this subject by stating that faculty who are comfortable with technology may lack the pedagogical skills that marry the technology to the content. Training is needed to support the instructional transition from instructor-centered to student-centered. Likewise, training is needed to assure that the technology is secondary to the content. Teaching at distance is not for every faculty but it should not be relegated to those with high levels of computer literacy. Providing faculty with personal technologies removes the fear of computer-mediated instruction. Providing the technical and instructional design support capitalizes on the delivery of the requested extrinsic rewards.

References:

Betts, K.S. (1998) George Washington University, Factors influencing faculty participation in distance eduction in postsecondary education in United States.

Bower, B. (2001) Online Journal of Distance Learning Administration.

Dillon, C. (1989) Faculty rewards and instructional telecommunications.

Dillion, C. & Walsh, S. (1999) Faculty; The neglected resource in distance education.

Draaves, W. (2002), Teaching Online.

Lenzer, R. (1997) Seeing things as they really are Forbes, 159 (5), March 10, 1997

Miller, J.T. (2000) Administrators, faculty and the final outcome in distance learning.

Moore, M. (2001) Distance Education in the United States.

Picciano, A.G,(2006) Educational Leadership and Planning for Technology, Fourth Edition.

Willis, B. (1994) Distance Education- Strategies and Tools and Distance Education.

http://www.westga.edu

http://www.yc.edu

Chapter 3: How to access additive fund in budget crisis?

Hardware Cost.

According to Ritchie and Boyle (1998) and Solomon (2001) that schools will have the budgets for technology that they want or need. Strategies for optimizing available funds include requiring competitive bids, scheduling hardware and software upgrades, using donated equipment, and using broken computers for spare parts.

Experts and teachers depend on their schools and district offices to take leadership in providing necessary resources, teacher input in this process is critically important. When schools and districts make hardware and software purchases, they are making curricular decisions. Therefore, it is important for purchases to begin with those that fulfill the curriculm needs for which teachers most need technology support (Ritchie and Boyle, 1998 and Soloman, 2001).

Schools have developed several arrangements to help ensure that computer equipment supports teachers' various curriculum needs. Schools can minimize technology repair problems if users follow good usage rules and conduct preventive maintenance procedures. In addition, education organizations usually choose one of the following maintenance options: maintenance contracts with outside suppliers, an in-house maintenance office, built-in maintenance budget. Each of these methods has its problems and limitations, and debate continues over which method or combination of methods is most cost effective depending on an organization's size and the number of computers and peripherals involved. Securing equipment is an equally important maintenance issue. Loss of equipment from vandalism and theft is a common problem in schools. Again, several options are available for dealing with this problem: monitoring and alarm systems, security cabinets, and lock-down systems (Ritchie and Boyle, 1998 and Solomon, 2001).

Fortunately and unfortunately, technology is constantly improving. It is fortunate because improvements in technology lead to more opportunities for integration in the classroom and to technology that is more aesthetically pleasing and user-friendly. However, as technology improves outside of the classroom walls, schools find that the computers that were new just four years ago are now running extremely slowly and cannot run the latest software programs. Thus, sustainability means that a plan for initial and sustained funding over time must be in place. School professionals must make wise choices related to when and how they spend technology funds (Ritchie and Boyle, 1998 and Solomon, 2001).

According to textbook the issue facing the district as it continues to get technology is whether to standardize its equipment for instructional applications. By using IBM technology the district could cuts cost and training cost. When the district set up programs, hardware, software and network for high school and middle schools students can be train for the workforce and summer programs at IBM.

E-IEP for special needs students like FAS/FAE was created by integrating assistive technology in the classroom (www.iowa-iep.net). Special education, more than other areas of education, is governed by laws and policies. This means that teachers, administrators, and special education technology specialists must be well versed in federal and state laws, policies, and procedures. To learn more about the legal and policy foundations of the field of special education technology, consult the following resources: Blackhurt (1997), Blackhurst and Edyburn (2000), U.S Department of Education (2000). Vincient A.S pears thinks that technologies have help his daughter cope in school and help her to learned reading technologies software, activities and construct activities. Students form their own knowledge and the relation between knowledge and reality (Bredo, 2000). Teaches teach student in the classroom, providing them with guidance as they move along in their learning technology activities and problem is the cost of the technology. A school cans apply for funding with Gates Foundation, IBM Program and Government grants.

References:

Picciano, A.G., (2006) Educational Leadership and Planning for Technology, Fourth Edition.

Roblyer, M.B, Doering, A.H., (2010) Integrating Educational Technology into Teaching, Fifth

Edition.

http://www.grants.gov

Case Study II Technology for all schools

According to Warschauer (2005/2006) ,Casey attended Mountain Springs HighSchool, which is

a large school mainly made up of students of the upper class status,while John attended Friendly

High School, a small rural school mainly composed of students lower to middle class status.

Casey is candidate for a college scholarship and he has many opportunities at Mountain Springs

High School for technology scholarships, like John who attends smaller school that does has

opportunity for technology scholarships. When Casey enrolled in the school in the ninth grade,

each student was issued a laptop computer to use for remainder of his or her high school career.

This was helpful to Casey in that it allows him to used software for writing, research, appling for

scholarships and science projects. But, John enrolled in the ninth grade at Friendly High School,

there was rarely time to use computer because there was one computer per grade level and one

lab that has 20 highly used computers. John's teacher is very technology and computer savvy and loves to learn and teach technology and computer. John 's classroom contains least 30 students that must shared the computer and computer lab but John could goes to the library for study hall and use the computer there and on weekend, John could goes to the public library to use the computer. John could ask his teacher to help him with his work. John is a smart student whom planed to attend college but he knows that his parents can not afford it. But, he can apply for grant, community scholarship and Gates Foundation Scholarship. John is jealous of Casey because of the technology and computer advantage at his school (Warschauer, Mark 2005/2006). According to court case Williams v. California (2004), which addressed the issue of educational quality that affected educational outcomes of poor students. Two basic issues were presented in this case: First, does the state of California provide all students the basic resources needed to learn such as qualified teachers, sufficient instructional materials, and adequate facilities? And second, should all students have a fundamental right to an equal education?

Williams, the plaintiff, argued that California's public education failed on both issues by not providing students the necessary educational resources, leading to unqual results across the schools in the state. Brown v.Board of Education was about separate but no equal, CFE v. State of New York was about accountability& funding reforms and Montoy v.State of Kansas, involving educational adequacy& state's school finance plan violates the state constitution [Essex, Nathan L.,(2008, 2005, 2002, 1999), School Law and the Public Schools, Fourth Edition, p.363.].

Renaissance Schools:

Barwell Road Elementary

Brentwood School of Engineering Magnet Elementary

Creek Road Elementary

Wilburn Elementary

Wake County Public School System received $10.2 million in funding from the Federal Race to the Top grant. The infusion of Race to the Top funding is an exciting opportunity for district to provide additional resources to schools to support raising academic achievement.

A portion of these funds will be used for our Renaissance Model. WCPSS developed the Renaissance Model to provide support for four of our elementary schools that will directly benefit from the extra resources provided by this grant.

Renaissance Schools offer a comprehensive range of opportunities:

Nationally recruited administration and faculty

Staff with a successful track record of student achievement

Innovative classrooms

Cutting-edge technology

Student enrichment programs during and after school

Starting with the 2011-2012 school year, classrooms in these four Renaissance Schools will have additional teaching staff for each grade level. In addition, these schools will have the flexibility to maximize instructional time during the school day (www.wcpss.net).

References:

Essex, Nathan L.,(2008, 2005, 2002, 1999), School Law and the Public Schools, Fourth Edition, p.363.

Warschaue Mark (2005/2006) Going one to one, Educational leadership p.34-38

Yudof Mark G., Kirp David L., Levin Betsy, Moran Rachel F.,(2002), Educational Policy and the Law, Fourth Edition, p.767.

http://www.edu/edtechcases

www.wcpss.net

Chapter 4: How to integrating educational technology into teaching and the classroom?

According to textbook: Educational leadership and Planning for Technology (Picciano, Anthony G.2006) ; Distance education is the term that has most commonly been used for several decades. A term for the physical separation of teachers and learners, where learners take on greater responsibility for their learning, as is frequently the case when doing so from a distance. Asynchronous: Happening at different times, communication is characterized by time-independence; that is, the sender and receiver do not communicate at the same time. An example is electronic mall (Picciano, 2006). Face to Face learning is in the classroom. Synchronous: Happening at the same time, communication is characterized by time-dependence; that is, the sender and receiver communicate at the same time. An example is a telephone conversation (Picciano, 2006).

Vincient A. Spears traveled to distance learning planets. The first planet was In See See You in 1976 to 1980 where he phscally attend education program of Criminal Justice (NCCU,1980, BA), then traveled to the planet of US Army (1980 to 1983, Medical Specialist), then traveled to planet of Correspondent Schools: ICS(Basic Computer Programmer) and Kensington University (Law School,2001,JD), where the distance learning was by mail, then planet of online schools (Capella University for only a year and Strayer University, learning on blackboard). Accorded to Dr.Angie Parker (Yavapai College, Distributed Learning), Colleges continue offer growing numbers of courses and programs of study through distance education technologies. At the millennium, the Association of Governing Boards of Universities and Colleges estimated that one-third of all colleges and universities would be closing with ten years.Accorded to Peter Drucker, a management theorist, recently predicted that higher education institution as we know them today will be relics in a matter of a few short years (Lenzer, 1997).

In addition to the need for change, is the need to work within new budgetary constraints being set forth by legislatures across the nation? These budget cuts are threatening to derail many traditional programs in higher education, forcing colleges and universities to look to faculty for cost saving distance delivery alternatives. Distance delivery has proven to be a means of recouping lost revenue, but without will faculty, the programs are destined for collapse. If distance education is not only to sustain itself but to grow in upcoming years, it is imperative for administrators to understand the motivation that entices faculty to transition to alternative delivery modes. A number of authors have taken on the task of investigating incentives which translslate into the distance learning paradigm (Betts, 1998; Rockwell, Schauer, Fritz & Marx, 1999; Wills, 1994; Wilson, 1998). The success of any future distance eduction program is hanged on enticing faculty to move their courses to distant formats. Flexible scheduling also allows a wider audience of potential learners to access instruction. Technology-mediated instuction can be accessed 24/7 from nearly any location, opening potential for working students, parents of young children, and those with disabilities to reach their educational goals. Moore (2001) relates that the advent of interactive media and flexible scheduling has also brought forth a new generation of distance faculty who are now able to teach while pursuing other intesests. Workload was also addressed from the perspective of class size. Class size policies are widely diverse and have a direct tie to the budget. Although numerous studies (Bower, 2001: Mckenzie,

Mims, Bennett & Waugh, 2002) present the incentive of smaller class sizes, colleges are reluctant to limit registrations. Faculty, on the other hand, question the quality of instruction with class loads exceeding twenty-five students.Draves (2000) suggests that class size policies remain consistent between online and traditional, while Miller (2000) suggests a sliding scale of stipends for faculty who teach courses in excess of twenty-five students. Dillon (1998) and Dillon and Walsh (1998) add to the literature on this subject by stating that faculty who are comfortable with technology may lack the pedagogical skills that marry the technology to the content. Training is needed to support the instructional transition from instructor-centered to student-centered. Likewise, training is needed to assure that the technology is secondary to the content. Teaching at distance is not for every faculty but it should not be relegated to those with high levels of computer literacy. Providing faculty with personal technologies removes the fear of comupter-mediated instruction. Providing the technical and instructional design support capitalizes on the delivery of the requested extrinsic rewards.

References:

Betts, K.S. (1998) Goerge Washington University, Factors influencing faculty participation in distance eduction in postsecondary education in United States.

Bower, B. (2001) Online Journal of Distance Learning Administration.

Dillon, C. (1989) Faculty rewards and instructional telecommunications.

Dillion, C. & Walsh, S. (1999) Faculty; The neglected resource in distance education.

Draaves, W. (2002), Teaching Online.

Lenzer, R. (1997) Seeing things as they really are Forbes, 159 (5), March 10, 1997

Miller, J.T. (2000) Administrators, faculty and the final outcome in distance learning.

Moore, M. (2001) Distance Education in the United States.

Picciano, A.G,(2006) Educational Leadership and Planning for Technology, Fourth Edition.

Willis, B. (1994) Distance Education- Strategies and Tools and Distance Education.

http://www.westga.edu

http://www.yc.edu

Multiple Intelligences in the Classroom (What is Multiple Intelligences Theory?)

According to Howard Gardner's theory of Multiple Intelligences utilizes aspects of cognitive and developmental psychology, anthropology, and sociology to explain the human intellect. Although Gardner had been working towards the concept of Multiple Intelligences for many years prior, the theory was introduced in 1983, with Gardner's book, Frames of Mind.

Gardner's research consisted of brain research and interviews with stroke victims, prodigies, and individuals with autism. Based on his findings, Gardner established eight criteria for identifying the seven (he has subsequently added an eighth and is considering a ninth) separate intelligences. The eight criteria used by Gardner to identify the intelligences are listed below:

1. Isolation by brain damage/neurological evidence

2. The existence of prodigies, idiot savants, and exceptional individuals

3. Distinguishable set of core operations

4. Developmental stages with an expert end state

5. Evolutionary history and plausibility

6. Susceptibility to encoding in a symbol system

7. Support from experimental psychological tasks

8. Support from psychometric research

For a more detailed look at these eight criteria, visit http://surfaquarium.com/MI/criteria.htm.

Originally, the theory accounted for seven separate intelligences. Subsequently, with the publishing of Gardner's Intelligence Reframed in 1999, two more intelligences were added to the list. The intelligences are Verbal/Linguistic, Logical/Mathematical, Visual/Spatial, Bodily-Kinesthetic, Musical, Interpersonal, Intrapersonal, Naturalistic, and Existential.

Gardner's theory challenges traditional, narrower views of intelligence. Previously accepted ideas of human intellectual capacity contend that an individual's intelligence is a fixed entity throughout his lifetime and that intelligence can be measured through an individual's logical and language abilities. According to Gardner's theory, intelligence encompasses the ability to create and solve problems, create products or provide services that are valued within a culture or society. Originally, the theory accounted for seven separate intelligences. Subsequently, with the publishing of Gardner's Intelligence Reframed in 1999, two more intelligences were added to the list. The nine intelligences are outlined in more detail in the section below. Listed below are key points of Gardner's theory:

1. All human beings possess all nine intelligences in varying degrees.

2. Each individual has a different intelligence profile.

3. Education can be improved by assessment of students' intelligence profiles and designing activities accordingly.

4. Each intelligence occupies a different area of the brain.

5. The nine intelligences may operate in consort or independently from one another.

6. These nine intelligences may define the human species.

Gardner, a Professor of Education at Harvard University, and other researchers and educators continue to work towards a more holistic approach to education through Project Zero. For more information on the projects and research involved in Project Zero, visit the website at http://www.pz.harvard.edu.

Although the theory was not originally designed for use in a classroom application, it has been widely embraced by educators and enjoyed numerous adaptations in a variety of educational settings Teachers have always known that students had different strengths and weaknesses in the classroom. Gardner's research was able to articulate that and provide direction as to how to improve a student's ability in any given intelligence. Teachers were encouraged to begin to think of lesson planning in terms of meeting the needs of a variety of the intelligences. From this new thinking, schools such the Ross School in New York, an independent educational institution, and the Key Learning Community, a public magnet school in Indianapolis emerged to try teaching using a Multiple Intelligences curriculum. The focus of this part of the chapter will be on lesson design using the theory of Multiple Intelligences, and providing various resources that educator's may use to implement the theory into their classroom activities. Ms. Cunningham, a seventh grade American History Teacher, is preparing a unit on the American Civil Rights Movement of the 1950's and 1960's. The teacher has created a succession of lessons to be completed over a two-week period to enhance her students' understanding of the events, organizations, and individuals that were crucial to the movement. When the unit is over, Ms. Cunningham wants her students to have a complete picture of the historical period. She designs a variety of activities that give the students the opportunity to explore historical and cultural aspects of the 1950's and 1960's, and to fully identify with those who were involved in the Movement. In order to reach her instructional goals, the students will read selected excerpts from the textbook and listen to various lecturers about the Movement. In addition to the aforementioned, the students will complete several exploratory tasks about the Civil Rights movement as well.

To begin the unit the teacher uses a KWL chart on the overhead to spur discussion and start the students' "juices" flowing. A KWL chart is visual representations of what students already know, what they want to know, and what they learned at the end of a lesson. This activity is completed as a class. The students take turns sharing the tidbits of information that they already know about the Civil Rights movement. This information is on major figures, events and places involved in the Civil Rights movement. Upon establishing what basic prior knowledge the students possess, it is now time to begin discovering new information and confirming previously held information about the Civil Rights movement. Ms. Cunningham then lectures on the basic events, people, and places involved in the majority of the Civil

Rights movement in order to provide students some framework within which to begin placing their new information.

She closes the first lesson by asking the students to create a timeline using the dates of events she has provided. This will be a working outline to be used throughout the unit. During a subsequent lesson, students are asked to share their outlines with their classmates in small groups. They should make corrections and comments on the outlines as needed. Ms. Cunningham gains class consensus of the proper order for their working outline as she places an enlarged version on the classroom wall.

The culmination of this unit will be a final project in which students create a portfolio containing work on three mini-projects. All students will listen to the same guest lecturers, view the same video taped footage and participate in the same class discussions during the first half of each class. The remainder of each class period will be reserved for work on personal exploration pertaining to their portfolio pieces. Ms. Cunningham has provided a list of possible activities and a rubric for each suggested activity in order to support and to guide the student's work. She has also arranged her room so that "art" materials are in a central location; mapping and graphing information is grouped together and there is a section replete with reading and research materials.

Mrs. Cunningham's students will have many options for creating something chat can be included in their portfolios. Students will have the option to write letters to members of the community who were teenagers during the Civil Rights Movement, asking them to share their memories and experiences about life during the time period. Students may work in teams to prepare speeches based on period issues for their fellow classmates. Students may consult with the school's Media Specialist or more knowledgeable other to find resources for the class, including popular music from the time period. They may also learn and share dances that were popular during the 1950's and 1960's. If they choose, students may include music in the plays they write and act out for their classmates. With the assistance of the Art instructor, students may opt to work together to create a mural that represents key figures of the Civil Rights Movement such as Rosa Parks and Martin Luther King Jr., with accompanying biographical information about each leader. Students may also create a map representing key events. Students may also work in groups to prepare short plays to enact for the class based on the readings and what they learn from the guest speakers. Afterwards, Mrs. Cunningham will moderate discussion sessions about the plays. All students will keep a record of their thoughts and feelings about the mini-lessons they completed. This journaling process will provide a synthesis of the materials with which they dealt. As one final measure, students present their portfolios to their classmates.

James, a student whose proclivities lean towards creative visual projects expresses interest in working on the mural of Civil Rights leaders. Mrs. Cunningham feels that James needs to shift gears and concentrate on other activities in the classroom. The teacher suggests that James work on creating the map and / or timeline. At the teacher's encouragement, James begins to work on the other projects, but his attention continues to drift towards the students painting the mural. He contributes some excellent ideas and shows so much interest in the details and creation of the mural, that the teacher allows him to shift his focus back towards the visual project.

In another seventh grade classroom, Mr. Smith taught a unit on the Civil Rights Movement by assigning textbook readings and lecturing the students on the historical events surrounding the Movement. Students were given sentence completion pop quizzes throughout the course of the lesson. The teacher showed videotaped programs to the class and each student wrote a short research paper about a Civil Rights leader or prominent figure. At the end of the unit, students were given a multiple choice and essay test.

There are many ways to incorporate Multiple Intelligences theory (Gardner, H. 1983) into the curriculum, and there is no set method by which to incorporate the theory. Some teachers set up learning centers with resources and materials that promote involving the different intelligences. For example, in the above scenario, Ms. Cunningham creates an area with art supplies in her classroom. Other instructors design simulations that immerse students into real life situations. Careful planning during the lesson design process will help to ensure quality instruction and valuable student experiences in the classroom.

Other instructional models, such as project-based and collaborative learning may be easily integrated into lessons with Multiple Intelligences. Collaborative learning allows students to explore their interpersonal intelligence, while project-based learning may help structure activities designed to cultivate the nine intelligences. For instance, Ms. Cunningham uses aspects of project-based learning in her classroom by allowing students to plan, create, and process (through reflection) information throughout the Civil Rights unit, while also integrating activities that teach to the intelligences. This particular instructional model allows students to work together to explore a topic and to create something as the end product. This works well with Multiple Intelligences theory, which places value on the ability to create products. By collaborating with the Media Specialist to give students the opportunity to choose from a variety of resources to complete their assignments, Ms. Cunningham uses aspects of resource-based learning, an instructional model that places the ultimate responsibility of choosing resources on the student.

It is important for teachers to carefully select activities that not only teach to the intelligences, but also realistically mesh with the subject matter of the lesson or unit. Multiple Intelligences theory should enhance, not detract from what is being taught.

Disney's website entitled Tapping into Multiple Intelligences suggests two approaches for implementing Multiple Intelligences theory in the classroom. One is a teacher-centered approach, in which the instructor incorporates materials, resources, and activities into the lesson that teach to the different intelligences. The other is a student-centered approach in which students actually create a variety of different materials that demonstrate their understanding of the subject matter. The student-centered approach allows students to actively use their varied forms of intelligence. In a teacher-centered lesson, the number of intelligences explored should be limited to two or three. To teach less than two is nearly impossible since the use of speech will always require the use of one's Verbal/Linguistic intelligence. In a student-centered lesson, the instructor may incorporate aspects of project-based learning, collaborative learning, or other inquiry-based models. In such a case, activities involving all nine intelligences may be presented as options for the class, but each student participates in only one or two of the tasks.

Ms. Cunningham incorporates both student-centered and teacher-centered activities into her unit on the Civil Rights Movement. The teacher-led lecture is a standard example of a teacher-centered activity. The lecture teaches to students' Verbal/Linguistic Intelligence. The viewing of the videotape is another example of a teacher-centered activity. This activity incorporates Visual/Spatial Intelligence into how the unit is learned. It is important to note that many activities, although designed to target a particular intelligence, may also utilize other intelligences as well. For example, in Ms. Cunningham's classroom the students may work together on creating a mural of Civil Rights Leaders. This is a student-centered activity that directly involves Visual/Spatial intelligence, but also gives students a chance to exercise their Interpersonal Intelligence. The journal assignment, also a student-centered activity, is designed to enhance students' Intrapersonal Intelligence by prompting them to reflect on their feelings and experiences in relation to the Civil Rights movement. This activity also taps into Verbal/Linguistic Intelligence. The timeline and map assignments are student-centered activities that are designed to enhance students' Logical/Mathematical Intelligence, but they also delve into Visual/Spatial Intelligence. Students must collect and organize information for both the timeline and the map therefore using their Logical/Mathematical intelligence. In creating these items, students must think visually as well. By incorporating dance into one lesson, Ms. Cunningham is able to promote awareness of her students' Bodily-Kinesthetic intelligence. By showing videos of popular dances from the time period, or inviting an expert from the community to talk about the social aspects of dance, Ms. Cunningham might incorporate a teacher-centered activity. Having students learn and perform dances is a student-centered way of teaching through Bodily-

Kinesthetic intelligence. The short plays that students prepare involve Bodily-Kinesthetic intelligence, as well as Interpersonal and Verbal/Linguistic intelligences. Class discussions provide an opportunity for students to exercise both areas of their personal intelligences, as well as to reinforce the subject matter.

Planning and Implementing Student-Centered Lessons

This type of lesson revolves around student created materials. The types of activities and assignments that support student-centered lessons can be easily designed in concert with many of the inquiry-based models discussed in the text of this book. One of the most important aspects of student-centered lessons is allowing students to make choices. Teachers should encourage students to exercise their weaker intelligences, but allow them to explore their stronger areas as well. In Ms. Cunningham's class, the student named James is very strong in Visual/Spatial Intelligence and always leans towards this type of project. The teacher encourages James to participate in other activities, but when it is obvious that his interest lies in working on the mural Ms. Cunningham allows him to work on the project.

Listed below are steps to implement a student-centered lesson or unit:

Carefully identify instructional goals, objectives, and instructional outcomes.

Consider activities that you can integrate into the lesson or unit that teach to the different intelligences. Teachers need not incorporate all nine intelligences into one lesson.

When gathering resources and materials, consider those which will allow students to explore their multiple intelligences.

Specify a timeframe for the lesson or unit.

Allow for considerable element of student choice when designing activities and tasks for the intelligences

Design activities that are student-centered, using inquiry-based models of instruction.

Provide a rubric for student activities. You might consider having students help create rubrics.

Incorporate assessment into the learning process.

In an effort to maximize students' interest in both the subject matter and their own learning proclivities, teachers may wish to teach their students a little bit about Multiple Intelligences. Teachers can brief the class about each type of intelligence and then follow up with a self-assessment for each student. In this way, students will be able to capitalize on their strengths and work on their weaker areas. Disney's Tapping into Multiple Intelligences website includes a self-assessment.

Planning and Implementing a Teacher-Centered Lesson

Structured, teacher-centered activities provide an opportunity for teachers to introduce material and establish prior knowledge and student conceptions. Teachers may lecture students, show informational videos and posters, perform drills, pose problem-solving exercises, arrange museum visits, and plan outings to concerts. There are all examples of teacher-centered activities. All of these activities integrate the Multiple Intelligences into the subject matter being taught. Teacher-centered lessons should be limited to a few activities that provide a foundation for students to later complete more exploratory tasks in which they can demonstrate understanding of the material. A teacher may choose to start an instructional unit or lesson with teacher-centered activities and then follow up with subsequent student-centered lessons. Teachers may follow these steps when designing and implementing a teacher-centered lesson:

Identify instructional goals and objectives

Consider teacher-centered activities that teach to students' Multiple Intelligences. In a teacher-centered lesson, limit the number of activities to two or three.

Consider what resources and materials you will need to implement the lesson. For example, will you need to schedule a museum visit or to consult the Media Specialist for videos or other media?

Specify a timeframe for the lesson or unit.

Provide an opportunity for reflection by students

Provide a rubric to scaffold student activities

Integrate assessment into the learning process

Assessment is one of the biggest challenges in incorporating Multiple Intelligences in the classroom. Ms. Cunningham's students are given the option of working on several mini-projects during the course of the Civil Rights unit. At the end of the unit, their performance is assessed through a portfolio that represents their work on these projects. It is very important for assessment to be integrated into the learning process. Assessment should give students the opportunity to demonstrate their understanding of the subject matter. One of the main goals of acknowledging and using Multiple Intelligences in the classroom is to increase student understanding of material by allowing them to demonstrate the ways in which they understand the material. Teachers need to make their expectations clear, and may do so in the form of a detailed rubric.

Benefits of Multiple Intelligences (Brandy Bellamy and Camille Baker, 2005)

Using Multiple Intelligences theory in the classroom has many benefits:

As a teacher and learner you realize that there are many ways to be "smart"

All forms of intelligence are equally celebrated.

By having students create work that is displayed to parents and other members of the community, your school could see more parent and community involvement.

A sense of increased self-worth may be seen as students build on their strengths and work towards becoming an expert in certain areas

Students may develop strong problem solving skills that they can use real life situations

Multiple Intelligences: Classroom Application (Table added by Brandy Bellamy and Camille Baker, 2005)

Table 2. *Multiple Intelligences: Classroom Application (Table added by Brandy Bellamy and Camille Baker, 2005)*

	Teacher Centered	Student Centered
Verbal/Linguistic	<ul><li>Present content verbally</li><li>Ask questions aloud and look for student feedback</li><li>Interviews</li></ul>	<ul><li>Student Presents Material</li><li>Students read content and prepare a presentation for his/her classmates</li><li>Students debate over an issue</li></ul>
Logical/Mathematical	<ul><li>Provide brain teasers or challenging questions to begin lessons.</li><li>Make logical connections between the subject matter and authentic situations to answer the question "why?"</li></ul>	<ul><li>Students categorize information in logical sequences for organization.</li><li>Students create graphs or charts to explain written info.</li><li>Students participate in web quests associated with the content</li></ul>
Bodily/Kinesthetic	<ul><li>Use props during lecture</li><li>Provide tangible items pertaining to content for students to examine</li><li>Review using sports related examples (throw a ball to someone to answer a question)</li></ul>	<ul><li>Students use computers to research subject matter.</li><li>Students create props of their own explaining subject matter (shadow boxes, mobiles, etc...)</li><li>Students create review games.</li></ul>
(cat)	When presenting the information, use visuals to explain content: PowerPoint Slides, Charts, Graphs, cartoons, videos, overheads, smart boards	<ul><li>Have students work individually or in groups to create visuals pertaining to the information:</li></ul>

Visual/Spatial		▪ Posters; timelines; models; power point slides; maps; illustrations, charts; concept mapping
Musical	▪ Play music in the classroom during reflection periods ▪ Show examples or create musical rythms for students to remember things	▪ Create a song or melody with the content embedded for memory ▪ Use well known songs to memorize formulas, skills, or test content
Interpersonal	▪ Be aware of body language and facial expressions ▪ Offer assistance whenver needed ▪ Encourage classroom discussion	▪ Encourage collaboration among peers ▪ Group work strengthens interpersonal connections ▪ Peer feedback and peer tutoring ▪ Students present to the class ▪ Encourage group editing
Intrapersonal	▪ Encourage journaling as a positive outlet for expression ▪ Introduce web logging (blogs) ▪ Make individual questions welcome ▪ Create a positive environment.	▪ Journaling ▪ Individual research on content ▪ Students create personal portfolios of work
	▪ Take students outside to enjoy nature while in learning process (lecture)	Students organize thoughts using natural cycles Students make relationships

Naturalistic	▪ Compare authentic subject matter to natural occurrences. ▪ Relate subject matter to stages that occur in nature (plants, weather, etc)	among content and the natural environment (how has nature had an impact?) Students perform community service

Learning Styles Section

Scenario

A group of four city planners in Boston is working on a project to improve the methods of repairing streets. They have spent a lot of time in the field looking at streets and learning about the stresses they receive, how engineers currently deal with those problems, and the public's perceptions of street conditions. Some improvements have been made including a new system of diagnosing problems and new methods of repairing the streets. The final stage of their project is to determine how to educate the city's employees on these improvements.

Jessica believes that showing maps of where the various sidewalks in various states of decay would be helpful. She also wants to use a flow chart to represent the new repair process. Maybe a computer instruction guide could be utilized in the employee education program.

Patrick feels that the planners need to discuss these improvements with the city's employees. A question and answer session could also be implemented in an attempt to answer any questions concerning the new system of diagnosing problems and new methods of repairing the streets.

Will has already begun work on an extensive training manual, which will provide a concrete resource to guide employees in training and for later reference. The manual will be available in hard copy and on the web.

Claire thinks that the city employees would benefit the most from a multimedia presentation as well as a CD-ROM with links to other useful information. She also wants the employees to go into the field and see some of the streets that were used as models in the new program. If that is not possible, pictures could be provided as examples to give the employees a concrete idea of the improvements.

Learning Styles

The term "learning styles" is commonly used throughout various educational fields and therefore, has many connotations. In general, it refers to the uniqueness of how each learner receives and processes new information through their senses. The National Association of Secondary School Principals defines learning style as, "the composite of characteristic cognitive, affective, and physiological factors that serve as relatively stable indicators of how a learner perceives, interacts with, and responds to the learning environment." Other phrases are used interchangeably with learning styles. Some include perceptual styles, learning modalities, and learning preferences (www.vark-learning.com).

Each person is born with certain preferences toward particular styles, but culture, experience, and development influence these preferences. The four most common learning styles are visual, aural, reading/writing, and kinesthetic/tactile. Most people learn through all modalities, but have certain strengths and weaknesses in a specific modality. Some people have an equal propensity for more than one style, which is titled as the multimodal style. This preference can be determined through various testing instruments. Once a person's learning style is ascertained, accommodations can be made to increase academic achievement and creativity, as well as improve attitudes toward learning.

The Visual Learning Style

Visual learners process information most effectively when the information is seen. Depictions can include charts, graphs, flow charts, and all the symbolic arrows, circles, hierarchies and other devices that instructors use to represent what could have been presented in worlds. These learners think in pictures and have vivid imaginations. Most people are classified as visual learners.

Jessica is a visual learner. Her suggestions focus on the use of visual aids to increase information processing.

The Aural Learning Style

Aural learners process information most effectively when spoken or heard. These learners respond well to lectures and discussions and are excellent listeners. They also like to talk and enjoy music and dramas. When trying to recall information, aural learners can often "hear" the way someone told them the information.

Patrick is an aural learner. His need to discuss the new improvements points to the benefits of obtaining information in an oral language format.

The Reading/Writing Learning Style

Reading/Writing learners process information most effectively when presented in a written language format. This type of learner benefits from instructors that use the blackboard to accent important points or provide outlines of the lecture material. When trying to recall information, reading/writing learners remember the information from their "mind's eye." Many academics have a strong preference for the reading/writing style.

Will is a reading/writing learner. His comprehensive training manual allows the employees to utilize the written language format.

The Kinesthetic/Tactile Learning Style

Kinesthetic/Tactile learners process information actively through physical means. Kinesthetic learning refers to whole body movement while tactile learning refers only to the sense of touch. These learners gesture when speaking, are poor listeners, and lose interest in long speeches. Most students that do not perform well in school are kinesthetic/tactile learners. The crux of this learning style is that the learner is connected to real situations through experience, example, practice, or simulation.

Claire is a kinesthetic/tactile learner. Her method of instruction utilizes "hands on" demonstrations and field experiences.

Learning Strategies for Each Learning Style

The Visual Learning Style

Replace words with symbols or initials.

Translate concepts into pictures and diagrams.

Underline or highlight your notes or textbooks with different colors.

Practice turning your visuals back into words.

Make flashcards of key information with words, symbols, and diagrams.

The Aural Learning Style

Attend lectures and tutorials.

Discuss topics with your instructor and other students.

Put summarized notes on tape and listen to them.

Join a study group or have a "study buddy."

Tape records your lectures.

When recalling information or solving problems, talk out loud.

The Reading/Writing Learning Style

Write out important information again and again.

Read your notes silently.

Organize any diagrams into statements.

Rewrite the ideas and principles in other words.

Make flashcards of words and concepts that need to be memorized.

The Kinesthetic/Tactile Learning Style

Sit near the instructor in classroom situations.

Read out loud from your textbook and notes.

Copy key points onto large writing surfaces (i.e. chalkboard or easel board).

Copy key points using word processing software.

Listen to audiotapes of your notes while exercising.

Take in information through field trips, laboratories, trial and error, exhibits, collections, and hands-on examples.

Put real life examples into your notes summary.

Recall experiments and role-play.

Use pictures and photographs that illustrate an idea.

Educational Implications for Learning Styles

Teachers that rely on learning styles have opened their classrooms to more than one approach to intellectual work. The activities planned by these teachers are more student-centered than traditional activities and have engaged in learning-style based instruction (Giles, E., Pitre, S., Womack, S. (2003), Multiple intelligences and learning styles. In M. Orey (Ed.), Emerging perspectives on learning, teaching, and technology).

The first step in implementing learning style-based instruction is diagnosing the individual learning styles of each student. A variety of methods exist for testing learning styles in a relatively quick manner. Many are available online, like the VARK Questionnaire listed above.

The second step is profiling group preferences and weaknesses. Are most of the students' visual learners? Does your class have very few kinesthetic/tactile learners?

The third step is assessing current instructional methods to determine whether they are adequate or require more flexibility. If modifications need to be made, various activities can be developed and/or adapted to conform with learning styles. Three techniques have been proposed.

1. Teachers can add alternative activities that could replace or supplement ones. This could create increased opportunities for students to use different styles. For example, hands on activities can be conducted after a lecture to confirm abstract concepts.

2. Teachers can also challenge students to develop skills in other areas by completing assignments that utilize all learning styles. For example, the students can complete multidimensional packets, which contain activities from each learning style.

3. Another approach to include learning styles in an education curriculum is to organize activities around complex projects. These projects would require that students use all learning styles. An example of a complex activity would be a project-based learning project.

When teaching an individual, teachers should present the most difficult concepts in the preferred style. Easier concepts should be introduced in a different style. When teaching an entire class, teachers should use all learning styles in their presentations if they are to reach every student. This can be fairly simple.

For example, Mrs. Erwin, a fifth grade teacher is going to teach a unit on Charlotte's Web. In order to accommodate all learning styles, she will have the students read sections of the book silently and out loud to others, act out various scenes, and complete a timeline of events on the bulletin board. Mrs. Erwin understands that students must be exposed to the concepts in a variety of ways to ensure full comprehension (http://projects.coe.uga.edu/epltt/)

Intelligence Area	Strengths	Preferences	Learns best through	Needs
Verbal / Linguistic	Writing, reading, memorizing dates, thinking in words,	Write, read, tell stories, talk, memorize,	Hearing and seeing words, speaking, reading,	Books, tapes, paper diaries, writing tools, dialogue, discussion,

	telling stories	work at solving puzzles	writing, discussing and debating	debated, stories, etc.
Mathematical/ Logical	Math, logic, problem-solving, reasoning, patterns	Question, work with numbers, experiment, solve problems	Working with relationships and patterns, classifying, categorizing, working with the abstract	Things to think about and explore, science materials, manipulative, trips to the planetarium and science museum, etc.
Visual / Spatial	Maps, reading charts, drawing, mazes, puzzles, imagining things, visualization	Draw, build, design, create, daydream, look at pictures	Working with pictures and colors, visualizing, using the mind's eye, drawing	LEGOs, video, movies, slides, art, imagination games, mazes, puzzles, illustrated book, trips to art museums, etc.
Bodily / Kinesthetic	Athletics, dancing, crafts, using tools, acting	Move around, touch and talk, body language	Touching, moving, knowledge	Role-play, drama, things to build, movement, sports and

			through bodily sensations, processing	physical games, tactile experience4s, hands-on learning, etc.
Musical	Picking up sounds, remembering melodies, rhythms, singing	Sing, play an instrument, listen to music, hum	Rhythm, singing, melody, listening to music and melodies	Sing-along time, trips to concerts, music playing at home and school, musical instruments, etc.
Interpersonal	Leading, organizing, understanding people, communicating, resolving conflicts, selling	Talk to people, have friends, join groups	Comparing, relating, sharing, interviewing, cooperating	Friends, group games, social gatherings, community events, clubs, mentors/ apprenticeships, etc.
Intrapersonal	Recognizing strengths and weaknesses, setting	Work alone, reflect pursue interests	Working alone, having space, reflecting, doing	Secret places, time alone, self-paced projects, choices, etc.

	goals, understanding self		self-paced projects	
Naturalistic	Understanding nature, making distinctions, identifying flora and fauna	Be involved with nature, make distinctions	Working in nature, exploring living things, learning about plants and natural events	Order, same/different, connections to real life and science issues, patterns

References

Armstrong, T. (1994). Multiple Intelligences in the classroom. Alexandria, VA: Association for Supervision and Curriculum Development.

Campbell, L., & Campbell, B. (1992). Teaching and learning through Multiple Intelligences. Seattle, WA: New Horizons for Learning.

Curry, Lynn. (1983). An organization of learning style theory and constructs. ERIC Document, 235, 185.

Dunn, R., and Dunn, K. (1978). Teaching students through their individual learning styles. Reston, VA: Reston Publishing Company, Inc.

Fogarty, R. (1997). Problem-based learning and other curriculum models for the Multiple Intelligences classroom. Arlington Heights, IL: IRI/Skylight Training and Publishing.

Gardner, H. (1983). Frames of mind: the theory of Multiple Intelligences. New York, NY: Basic Books.

Gardner, H. (1999). Intelligence reframed: Multiple Intelligences for the 21st century. New York, NY: Basic Books.

Zhang, Li-Fang. (2002). Thinking styles: Their relationships with modes of thinking and academic performance. Educational Ps

Websites:

Concept to Classroom: Cooperative and Collaborative Learning

Concept to Classroom: Tapping into Multiple Intelligences

Education World: Multiple Intelligences: A Theory for Everyone

Gardner's Eight Criteria for Identifying Multiple Intelligences

Integrated Learning Systems – The New Slavery by Gary S. Stager

These are curious times for public education in the United States. While millions of children suffer in our nation's schools, hordes of educators and corporate pitchmen are declaring themselves futurists – the person with the perfect solution for all of our educational ills. Too often the message of these emerging leaders is accompanied by a package of services or product to be purchased by schools in search of the miracle cure. For many of these "experts" technology is the key to educational reform. While I agree that new technologies will play a vital role in creating future learning cultures, the uses of technology often prescribed by the pundits are predicated upon misguided notions of behaviorism, drill, and expensive teaching machines. Unfortunately, many of our educational leaders equate educational restructuring with *plugging kids into anything that plugs in.* The ultimate result being "the injection of more misery into a school day which is already far too miserable for far too many students" (Kozol, J., 1992). There may be no better example of insensitive educational policy, unnecessary spending, or inappropriate use of technology than the proliferation of integrated learning systems.

One cans agree that new technology is equal way of measuring all stundents' works. District and state-adopted academic standard increased emphasis on educational accountability in the 1990s caused states to set curriculum standards and to create test to measure students' progress on them. Integrated software and management assessments aligned with these standards helps schools prepare for meeting these standards.

Accountability requirements of the No Child Left Behind Act stipulated that schools who fail to meet Adequate Yearly Progress for 3 years in a row must use a portion of their Title I funds for out-of-school tutoring, which the NCLB Act refers to as Supplemental Educational Services. ILS materials are ideal for providing these services (Readers' Choice Awards, 2004).

Broward County should be ashamed of themselves for their obscenely reckless and irresponsible expenditure of $13.5 million on integrated learning systems. In an age of scarce financial resources, troubled students, deteriorating school facilities, and outdated curricula, county bureaucrats decided to invest in Orwellian technology rather than kids. One might ask how school libraries, music, and art programs are faring in Broward County. How many disenfranchised students will stay in school because of the ILSs? How many others will drop out because of the lowered expectations and reduced human contact? In my opinion, the money would have been better spent buying the students lots of crack cocaine and passing out job applications for a lifetime career in local fast food restaurants.

The cost of technology is not cheap and it will not reduct class size. At Wake County Public Schools, they use the new technology like SPAN (Student Parent Access Network) and blackboard. This will cost money to operate it and update it like Strayer University.

The costs of ILSs conters on their expense as compareed to their impact on improving learning. ILS proponents feel that the students who experience the most success with ILSs are those whose needs are typically most difficult to meet (Becker, 1994; Bender, 1991; Bracy, 1992; Shore& Johnson, 1992).

The harsh metaphor between ELS installations and the drug trade is deliberate due to several similarities in the process of selling drugs and selling ILSs. First of all, the claims of educational euphoria made by ELS manufacturers are at best exaggerated. All of society's ills and educational shortcomings can be erased by hard-wiring students to integrated learning systems. You can buy thousands of prepared lessons, for all grade levels, interests, subject areas, and levels of difficulty in one package. The absurdity of this claim may be revealed by asking a group of teachers, "How long does it take you to perfect a lesson? How long would it take you to perfect thousands of lessons? How long would it take to communicate the subtleties of those thousands of lessons to a team of software designers?" Other claims along these lines suggest that "kids will like it" and test scores (the very same ones that every educator of conscience – even ETS themselves argue against) will rise. Henry Jay Becker's recent research on the research claims of the major ILSs provides convincing evidence of how shabby the DLS research actually is. Other research demonstrates that any gains in basic skills are short-lived, lacking in context, and are likely to widen the gap between the average and the remedial students because the remedial student spends his/her time drilling disjointed facts while their peers are more likely to be engaged in more creative and intellectually stimulating activities. Students need to have a balance of technology and non-technology programs education. An ILS system can be expensive for single classroom use, but a whole school district might determine that it has value in helping students learn (www.prenshall.com/ smaldino).With schools currently refousing their priorities on meeting standards in content areas and increasing scores on state and national tests,programs like health instruction and physical education have suffered. This is unfortunate, because three out of four deaths are due to preventable chronic conditions (U.S. Department of Health and Human Services, 1996). In addition, cognitive functioning is related to proper nutrition and physical activity (Caine& Caine, 1995). Also, children's concept and self-esteem (Payne & Issacs, 1995),as well as their prosocial skills (Borba, 1989),are positively affected by their involvement in physical activities.

Integrated Learning System companies disproportionately choose states with large populations of rural and urban socioeconomically disadvantaged students for their marketing. Many of these states have centralized decision-making where purchasing decisions are made by detached bureaucrat and politicians. It should come as no surprise that states like New Jersey with 600+ independent school districts have a much lower number of ILSs than more centralized states (or counties). Monetarily and/or educationally disadvantaged district administrators are made to feel intimidated and guilty for "denying their students access to cutting-edge technology and thereby reducing their students prospects for a successful life" if they don't install an ILS. Are academically successful, well-financed, pedagogically secure school districts or poor, disadvantaged, desperate school districts likely to embrace the ILS message?

Integrated Learning Systems often cause an unwelcome cycle of financial dependency. The painful expense of installing an ILS is disguised by the ILS representatives through a myriad of deferred payment strategies designed to give the impression of "something-for-noting." Sales are closed with small down payment/high interest lease-purchasing plans, wining and dining of administrators and politicians, "free" trials, and by interfering with the process of local educational decision- making. How many teachers are approached by the ILS proponents for their input? There are legions of horror stories in which the counsel of school principals, teacher unions, and computer coordinators is ignored by politicians or state department officials enticed by the purveyors of ILSs.

While a generation of children log-in at three and out at eighteen, future generations of illiterate Americans will be paying the debt incurred by the purchase of integrated learning systems. Buy the cool multimedia encyclopedia set-up for $1-2,000 and then the truck backs up with an ILS lab to be paid for into perpetuity.

References

Kozol, J. (1992). Savage inequalities: Children in America's schools. New York, NY: HarperPerennial.

Roblyer, M.D, and Doering,A.H.,(2010), Integrating Educational Technology into Teaching, Fifth Edition.

Sager, G. S. (1992). Integrated learning systems – The new slavery. Retrieved fromhttp://stager.tv/blog/?p=864 .

Smaldino, S.E., Lowther, D.L., and Russell, J.D., (2008),Instructional Technology and Media for Learning, Ninth Edition.

www.prenhall.com/smalino

www.wcpss.net

Chapter 5: How to train teachers and school leaders in technology in the classroom?

The harsh metaphor between ELS installations and the drug trade is deliberate due to several similarities in the process of selling drugs and selling ILSs. First of all, the claims of educational euphoria made by ELS manufacturers are at best exaggerated. All of society's ills and educational shortcomings can be erased by hard-wiring students to integrated learning systems. You can buy thousands of prepared lessons, for all grade levels, interests, subject areas, and levels of difficulty in one package. The absurdity of this claim may be revealed by asking a group of teachers, "How long does it take you to perfect a lesson? How long would it take you to perfect thousands of lessons? How long would it take to communicate the subtleties of those thousands of lessons to a team of software designers?" Other claims along these lines suggest that "kids will like it" and test scores (the very same ones that every educator of conscience – even ETS themselves argue against) will rise. Henry Jay Becker's recent research on the research claims of the major ILSs provides convincing evidence of how shabby the DLS research actually is. Other research demonstrates that any gains in basic skills are short-lived, lacking in context, and are likely to widen the gap between the average and the remedial students because the remedial student spends his/her time drilling disjointed facts while their peers are more likely to be engaged in more creative and intellectually stimulating activities. Students need to have a balance of technology and non-technology programs education. An ILS system can be expensive for single classroom use, but a whole school district might determine that it has value in helping students learn (www.prenshall.com/ smaldino).With schools currently refousing their priorities on meeting standards in content areas and increasing scores on state and national tests,programs like health instruction and physical education have suffered. This is unfortunate, because three out of four deaths are due to preventable chronic conditions (U.S. Department of Health and Human Services, 1996). In addition, cognitive functioning is related to proper nutrition and physical activity (Caine& Caine, 1995). Also, children's concept and self-esteem (Payne & Issacs, 1995), as well as their prosocial skills (Borba, 1989),are positively affected by their involvement in physical activities.

Integrated Learning System companies disproportionately choose states with large populations of rural and urban socioeconomically disadvantaged students for their marketing. Many of these states have centralized decision-making where purchasing decisions are made by detached bureaucrat and politicians. It should come as no surprise that states like New Jersey with 600+ independent school districts have a much lower number of ILSs than more centralized states (or counties). Monetarily and/or educationally disadvantaged district administrators are made to feel intimidated and guilty for "denying their students access to cutting-edge technology and thereby reducing their students prospects for a successful life" if they don't install an ILS. Are academically successful, well-financed, pedagogically secure school districts or poor, disadvantaged, desperate school districts likely to embrace the ILS message?

Integrated Learning Systems often cause an unwelcome cycle of financial dependency. The painful expense of installing an ILS is disguised by the ILS representatives through a myriad of deferred payment strategies designed to give the impression of "something-for-noting." Sales are closed with small down payment/high interest lease-purchasing plans, wining and dining of administrators and politicians, "free" trials, and by interfering with the process of local educational decision- making. How many teachers are approached by the ILS proponents for their input? There are legions of horror stories in which the counsel of school principals, teacher unions, and computer coordinators is ignored by politicians or state department officials enticed by the purveyors of ILSs.

While a generation of children log-in at three and out at eighteen, future generations of illiterate Americans will be paying the debt incurred by the purchase of integrated learning systems. Buy the cool multimedia encyclopedia set-up for $1-2,000 and then the truck backs up with an ILS lab to be paid for into perpetuity.

References

Kozol, J. (1992). Savage inequalities: Children in America's schools. New York, NY:

HarperPerennial.

Roblyer, M.D, and Doering, A.H., (2010), Integrating Educational Technology into

Teaching, Fifth Edition.

Sager, G. S. (1992). Integrated learning systems – The new slavery. Retrieved

from http://stager.tv/blog/?p=864 .

Smaldino, S.E., Lowther, D.L., and Russell, J.D., (2008),Instructional Technology and

Media for Learning, Ninth Edition.

www.prenhall.com/smalino

www.wcpss.net

Chapter 6: Summary:

Your principal has asked you to explain why the structure of knowledge is critical in quality curriculum design and instruction. Also, give him at least three insightful reasons to support concept-base curriculum and instruction.

1. How would you vompare education framed by the ideal of intellectual character and dispositions and education framrd by a set academic standards cover? How can you meet the intent of academic standards without sacrificing the development of intellectual charcter?

3. How would you explain the different levels in the Structure of Knoledge to a new teacher in your building?

4. As a teacher what oblidations do you have to help your students meet standard expeectations? Explain.

5. The standards movement is increasing stress on students and teachers. In what specific way schools and school districts help students and teachers manage the stress.

Teachers and students are facing challenges in the school system with the state budget. Schools must apply for Federal, state, local and foundations grant.

Vincient A. Spears visited his adoptive daughter's 7th grade class on 01-05-2010, talked about the blind students at Governor Morehead School where Vincient A. Spears works and encourage the students at North Garner Middle School to visit the school for the blind.

As, presentator begans with how it would feel like if you were blind? Had the students to close their eyes and walk around the classroom then had to opening their eyes and told me how it felt when their eyes were closed?

Variables:

Exercises: Toy Bear that is use to teach younger child or children with sight or without sight to tired shoe, button up clothes and zip up clothes. Told the students at NGMS (www.wcpss.net) to closed their eyes and try button up, zipup and tired the shoes of the toy bear.

Next topic was on Braille System: Students of NGMS are like most people; have a general idea of what Braille is. You know that blind individuals read Braille with their fingers. You even have wondered how anyone could read all of those dots. Let's find out! Let's go a little deeper and really learn what makes Braille work (Beginning Braille Transcription: Instructor: Dixie Mahaffie, http://www.ed2go.com/cgi-bin/classroom/getless.cig?c=bb&s=1009&lsn=01&chp=2).

The whole Braille system is based on six dots. The dots are arranged in two columns, two dots across and three dots down. This unit of six dots is called a Braille cell. Vincient A. Spears encouraged the students to learn more about blind students by visiting Governor Morehead School in Raleigh, NC.

In a wide sense, microlearning can be understood as a metaphor which refers to micro aspects of a variety of learning models, concepts and processes.

"No matter if learning refers to the process of building up and organizing knowledge, to the change of behavior, of attitudes, of values, of mental abilities, of cognitive structures, of emotional reactions, of action patterns or of societal dimensions, in all cases we have the possibility to consider micro, meso and macro aspects of the various views on more or less persisting changes and sustainable alterations of performances."

Depending on frames and domains of reference, micro, meso and macro aspects vary. They are relational concepts. For example, in the context of language learning, one might think of micro aspects in terms of vocabularies, phrases, sentences, and distinguish them from situations and episodes (meso aspects) and socio-cultural specifics or complex semantics (macro aspects). In a more general discourse on learning, one might differentiate between the learning of individuals, group learning or learning of organizations and the learning of generations or societies.

According to text book:"Concept-Based Curriculum and Instruction (Erickson Lynn H., copyright 2002 by Corwin Press, Inc.); to develop increasing sophistication in critical content knowledge, decisions have to be made about what is truly" critical." Correlating critical content topics at each grade level with key concepts to be developed shows the conceptual structure of the diffent disciplines (p.61).

Originally, the theory accounted for seven separate intelligences. Subsequently, with the publishing of Gardner's Intelligence Reframed in 1999, two more intelligences were added to the list. The intelligences are Verbal/Linguistic, Logical/Mathematical, Visual/Spatial, Bodily-Kinesthetic, Musical, Interpersonal, Intrapersonal, Naturalistic, and Existential.

Gardner's theory challenges traditional, narrower views of intelligence. Previously accepted ideas of human intellectual capacity contend that an individual's intelligence is a fixed entity throughout his lifetime and that intelligence can be measured through an individual's logical and language abilities. According to Gardner's theory, intelligence encompasses the ability to create and solve problems, create products or provide services that are valued within a culture or society. Originally, the theory accounted for seven separate intelligences. Subsequently, with the publishing of Gardner's Intelligence Reframed in 1999, two more intelligences were added to the list. The nine intelligences are outlined in more detail in the section below. Listed below are key points of Gardner's theory:

1. All human beings possess all nine intelligences in varying degrees.

2. Each individual has a different intelligence profile.

3. Education can be improved by assessment of students' intelligence profiles and designing activities accordingly.

4. Each intelligence occupies a different area of the brain.

5. The nine intelligences may operate in consort or independently from one another.

6. These nine intelligences may define the human species.(http://www.pz.harvard.edu).

According to the book"VICTORY IN OUR SCHOOLS"(Major Gereral Stanford,John.Army(Ret),Superintendent of Seattle Public Schools with Simons

Robin,forewold by Vice President Al Gore, 1999),The first step in building our achievement system was determining what we want our children to learn. The standards seemed to vary from class to class.We needed a stronger curriculm, which would encourage children to analyze information, evealuateit, and apply it to their lives (Stanford 1999, p.32). At Governor Morehead School for the Blind, they more life skills students than academic.

Depending on frames and domains of reference, micro, meso and macro aspects vary. They are relational concepts. For example, in the context of language learning, one might think of micro aspects in terms of vocabularies, phrases, sentences, and distinguish them from situations and episodes (meso aspects) and socio-cultural specifics or complex semantics (macro aspects). In a more general discourse on learning, one might differentiate between the learning of individuals, group learning or learning of organizations and the learning of generations or societies.

Furthermore, microlearning marks a transition from common models of learning towards micro perspectives on and the significance of micro dimensions in the process of learning. The microlearning approach is an emergent paradigm, so there are no hard definitions or coherent uses of the term yet. However, the growing focus on microlearning activities can be seen by web users' activities on the subject, who tag their corresponding weblog postings and social bookmarks with the term 'microlearning'.

As an instructional technology, microlearning focuses on the design of micro learning activities through micro steps in digital media environments, which already is a daily reality for today's knowledge workers. These activities can be incorporated in learner's daily routines and tasks. Unlike "traditional" e-learning approaches, microlearning often tends towards push technology through push media, which reduces the cognitive load on the learners. Therefore, the selection of micro learning objects and also pace and timing of micro learning activities are of importance for didactical designs (www.k12academics.com/educational-psychology/**micro**learning/introduction).

BEAR Assessment: 1.Assessment should be based on a developmental perspective of student learning. 2. What is taught and what is assessed must be clearly aligned. 3. Teachers are the managers and users of assessment data. And 4.Classroom assessment must uphold sound standards of validity and reliability (The Obama Education Plan, Copyright 2009, p.26, BAS; Wilson&Sloan, 2000). Expectations about what all students should learn- and, by implication, what they should be tested on-have changed in response to social, economic, and technological changes and as a result of the standards-base reform movement. Standards-based reform has increased both the amount of testing and the stakes attached to test results. This development has placed more pressure on current assessment systems than they were meant to bear (EDU510 Educational Assessment). Over thirty years of research have documented that talking; reading, spelling, and writing are integral processes that begin in the earliest years of life. These are ways children learn to use language to express and receive ideas and to share in the meaning of their worlds. Their use of oral and written language develops as they learn to speak and are involved in the daily routines of family life. Gradually, children build up practical knowledge, gained through everyday talk with family members and peers, which serves as the foundation of reading and writing. In turn, the nature of the practical knowledge children acquire is very much influenced by family and peers, along with ethnic, socioeconomic, regional, and cultural factors. The course of children's literacy and multiple literacy development is shaped by parental support for talking, reading, spelling, and writing; parents' approaches to reading and writing, and expectations; and the congruence between home and school linguistic environments in the early years of schooling accorded by Scarborough (1998).

We know from scientifically-based research that some early language and literacy concepts and skills are strong predictors of later reading achievement[1]. For example, phonological awareness, the ability to distinguish the sounds in language distinct from meaning, is a strong predictor of future reading. This means that educators can use phonological awareness data collected in kindergarten as a window to how well children are likely to read at the end of first grade stated by Scarborough (1998). This prediction of later achievement based on the current level of performance is referred to as a trajectory. Other strong predictors of reading achievement are letter identification and verbal memory for stories and sentences. It is important, therefore, to assess often children's early reading concepts and skills and to use that information to teach explicitly and systematically the concepts and skills to develop children into strong readers and writers. Skilled teaching can alter a student's trajectory, from one of not likely to read on grade level at the end of third grade to actually reading at or above grade level by the end of the third grade. Wake County Public Schools have setup pre-test at the beginning of the school year, to work on the area the students are weak on.

———————————————

Vincient A.Spears travels through the pages of this article" Stand By Me", the learner began to

wonder how do teachers cope with all the pressures of teaching? In Florida seemed the teachers

are bellwether about the bonuses and merit pay. When the Department of Education announced

the bonuses system and the exceptional teachers can apply for the bonuses 4out of Pasco

County's 3,600 teachers applied for the bonuses program. Standards, testing and accountability

is the latest venue where, according to teachers, too many student ratio to teachers in the

classrooms and not enough support. The teachers believe in higher standard but do not believe in

standardize test playing the great part, it playing now. Where students and teachers spent a lot of

times preparing for the test like the end the grade test in N.C.; when the students failed the test

then the teachers are held accountability. The election2008 some blamed the teachers for our

failing schools (Stand By Me p9 and 11)."Education is what survives when what has been

learned has been forgotten" (B.F.Skinner, New Scientist, May 12, 1964). The relationships a

child develops in school become critical to his or her positive development. Because of the

amount of time children spend in school, the relationships fostered there carry real weight (cited

in Family American, 1990).Also children may for the first time be developing relationships with

adults outside their home and family. These connection help a child develop cognitively and

emotionally (www.bronfenbrenner.com). This makes the teaching harder as the article stated

seventy-six percent of those surveyed believe teachers have become "the scapegoats for all the

problems facing education."Parents aren't the only ones who let them (teachers) down. For

example 2/3(67%) of new teachers have reported that their own school often or sometimes puts

obstacles in the way of accomplishing their goals. Absent Parents are parents that will not teach

and hold their children accountable (Stand By Me p.12).Dr.Bill Crosby stated that parents need to do homework with their children, have teachers and parents conferences and joined the PTA. President Elect Obama said the same thing, this learner agreed with the teachers, Dr.Bill Crosby and President Obama about AWOL Parents. The children have no respect for the teachers and each other. Teachers are concerned about disrespectful, unruly, rude students in the focus groups for the Stand By Me article, students walk around through the halls, in the classrooms and cursing and do whatever they want. This learner believes when they took prayer out of the school a lot of this are going around because the Golden Ruler is a prayer. Despite the myriad of obstacles teachers come up against, almost 2in 3(65%) say they believe that truly good teachers can overcome societal barriers such as poverty or uninvolved parents and still get their students to learn what they are supported to (Stand By Me p.16). The movies the "Ron Clark Story, Lean on Me and Sister Act 2 shown how to reach the students. This learner believes that all teachers can be good teachers if they get the support from the schools, government and parents. Money is an issue of teachers. N.Y. (CNNMoney.com)—Jonathan Hash, a history teacher at Herbert Hoover High School in San Diego, was enthusiastic about the teaching career he began two years ago. But now he might lose his job because of the statewide budget crisis, and that could force him to leave teaching altogether. Hash loved to teach but makes $43,000.00 a years and just brought a home with his pregnant wife in one of the nation's most expensive housing markets. Hash is considering joining family members in real estate or insurance (CNNMONEY.com). Pay for performance was cover in the article "Stand by Me". As things stand now, newcomers are notably more optimistic about merit pay. They may be more entrepreneurial in their view about work, or perhaps they are just on the lookout for ways to raise their own pay without waiting for the years to add up. Whatever the basis, a majority of new teachers(55%) think districts should be able to use other criteria-besides years of experience and education-to financially reward good teachers(compared with 33% of veterans). They also are more likely to think merit pay could be effectively used as a carrot for recruiting "the best and the brightest "into the profession (39% vs. 23%). Asked what they think would be more likely to happen if merit pay were actually implemented at their own school, beginners seem less concerned than veterans about potential downside, such as the possibility of a decline in teacher camaraderie (54% vs. 67%) or principals playing favorites (41% vs. 55%)(Stand By Me p.33). This learner knows about merit pay which does has its favorites when come to the job performance. While more than 8 in 10 teachers are union members, veteran teachers are far more likely to be attacked to their union. By to large margins, veteran teachers are more likely to consider the union to be absolutely essential (57% vs. 30%) and to be actively engaged in union activities (46% vs. 20%)(Stand By Me p.34). Most teachers are a member of the National Education Association that represents 3.2 million education professional nationwide. The teachers are face with budget cuts which could result in lost jobs and early retirement. This is a crisis that this learner is facing as state employee and if we lose our teachers to the crisis, who will teach?

References:

Desimone, L., Finn-Stevenson, M., and Henrich, C. (200) Whole School Reform In A Low-Income African American Community: The Effects Of The CoZi Model On Teachers, Parents, And Students. Urban Education, 35 (3), 269-323.

Addison, J.T. (1992). Urie Bronfenbrenner. Human Ecology, 20(2), 16-20.

Pellegrino James W., Chudowsky Naomi, and Glaser Robert, Knowing what Students Know, Copyright 2001

Starkey P. and Klein, A. (2000) Fostering Parental Support For Children's Mathematical Development: An Intervention With Head Start Families. Early Education and Development, 11 (5), 659-680.

The Obama Education Plan, Copyright 2009, Published by Jossey-Bass.

Hui T.Keung, 2009 July 13, Calendars may thwart transfers, THE NEWS&OBSERVER, p.b1

Scientifically-based research claims refer to those that have published findings in refereed journals (scientific publications that employ a process of peer review), duplication of results by other investigators, and consensus within a particular research community on whether there is a critical mass of studies that point toward a particular conclusion (Stanovich & Stanovich, 2003, p.6).

Concept-Based Curriculm and Instruction (Erickson Lynn H., Forword by Tomlinson Carol Ann, copyright 2002 by Corwin Press, Inc.).

VICTORY IN OUR SCHOOLS (Major General Stanford John,Army[Ret],Superintendent of Seattle Public Schools,1999).

Wadsworth Deborah,Article "Stand By Me"

www.ronclarkstory.com

www.wcpss.net

www.cnnmoney.com/teachers

www.bearcent.berkeley.edu

Stage of life and Rights of Vincient A. Spears

Children need to begin asserting control and power over the environment. Success in this stage of life (Initiative vs. Guilt) leads to sense of purpose (Erikson's Psychosocial Stage of Development). The learner(Vincient A. Spears) traveled back in his time machine when he was 5 year old in 1963 when he past by park car with two young white boys(ages 4 and 5) in it, the learner got near the car and the boys called the learner a" nigger" (Dunn,NC 1963). When the learner got home, the told his parents about what he was call as he walked to downtown. The learner's father said "You are not a nigger but a proud Negro boy and the learner's mother said that "GOD have no color and GOD loves you and created you" and his mother talked about the trial of Jesus: The soldiers led Jesus away into the palace(that is, the Praetorium)and called together the whole company of soldiers. They put a purple robe on him, the twisted together a crown of thorns and set it on him. And they began to call out to him."Hail, king of the Jews (Mark 15:16-20, Holy Bible)!"Again and again they stuck him on the head with a staff and spit on him. Falling on their knees, they paid homage to him. And when they had mocked him, they took off the purple robe and put clothes on him. Then they led him out to crucify him (The New Testament, Holy Bible, p.1095). Then the learner' s father told him about the time he (the father) went to bar with his Army friends and ordered some drinks , the owner came out and said "We do not serve niggers in here". Then , the learner's father said "I am glad you do not serve nigger in here because I do not want a nigger but a beer"(Eugene Spears one the first black male in the Special Force 82nd Airborne). This learner learned about life in the south and civil right. The learner felt guilt about being black and in later years ,the learner remember the song" Said it out loud I' m black and I'm proud" and the movie" Remember The Titan". The learner was taught about GOD and JESUS at a young age and to pray to GOD for help and to talk to the parents about anything, he needs .Children who try to exert too much power experience disapproval, resulting in sense of guilt (Erik Erikson' s Psychosocial Stage of Development). Kohlberg's Moral Development (1963) concepts of consecutive stages are rich with theological implications. Then, Vincient A. Spears traveled to Raleigh, NC on Nov. 5, 2008, when some white students (NCSU) wrote and drew in the University's Free Expression Tunnel:" Let's shoot that n—in the head" and "Hang Obama by a Noose." There also were references to the Ku Klux Klan. U.S Secret Service, which determined the painting were not a serious threat against

President-elect Barack Obama's life (Locke Mandy and Friedman Leah, Staff Writers, News& Observer, Nov.20, 2008).But black students did not feel that safe and Vincient A. Spears' a black learner at Strayer University and live in Raleigh, NC , felt that past was repeating itself. Vincient A. Spears got back into the time machine and traveled to Harnett Jr. High School, where a teacher punished him by making him put his nose in circle that was draw on a blackboard. This was cruel and unusual punishment which inflicted such pain of emotions that he could not bear at those times which cause Vincient A. Spears to become quiet and he had to overcome his pain from that punishment. The question of the constitutionality of corporal punishment was reaffirmed in the landmark case Ingraham v.Wright, where the U.S. Supreme Court ruled that even severe corporal punishment may not violate the Eighth Amendment prohibition of cruel and unusual punishment. This case arose when Ingraham and another student from the Dale County, Florida, and public schools filed suit after they had been subjected to paddling. State law allowed corporal punishment if it was not "degrading or unduly severe (School Law and the Public Schools, Fourth Edition, Essex Nathan L.P.76-79) and if it was done after consultation with the principal or other teacher in charge of the school. Paddling was considered a less drastic form of punishment than suspension. For violating a teacher's instruction, Ingraham had received twenty licks while he was held over a table in the principal's office. He required medical attention and missed school for several days. Because this paddling was probably "unduly severe," the high court hearing the evidence and appeals found no constitutional violation. According to Justice Powell," The schoolchild has little need for the protection of the Eighth Amendment." It is more appropriately applied in the case of the criminally convicted and thereby involuntarily confined.

While the court declined to declare corporal punishment as used in the context of public schools to be a violation of the cruel and unusual proscription or due process under federal law, it did state that paddling students deprived them of liberty interests protected by the Constitution. Although not required by law, but in the spirit of fairness, rudimentary due process should be applied before corporal punishment is administered. In spite of the ruling, federal courts have subsequently ruled that excessive corporal punishment violates the substantive due process clause of the Fourteenth Amendment. The courts, however, have fallen short of determining exactly when corporal punishment becomes excessive (p.79).

Although the Ingraham case upholds the legality of corporal punishment as an acceptable means of controlling student behavior, local school district policy in many cases have seriously limited use.

Kohlberg 's theory is especially relevant to current discussions of the gospel (Holy Bible: Four Books of JESUS the CHRIST 's life), the atonement, the Law, Comments and the true character of GOD the father and JESUS the son (John 3:16, Holy Bible).An application of his theory to the story of GOD's dealing with ancient children of Israel, offers a rational explanation of actions on GOD 's part which may seem harsh or unduly severe from our perspective. Stage 1: PUNISHMENT AND OBEDIENCE: Avoidance of physical punishment and deference to power. Punishment is an automatic response of physical retaliation. The immediate physical consequences of an action determine its goodness or badness. The atrocities carried out soldiers during the holocaust who were simply" carrying out orders" under threat of punishment, illustrate that adults as well as children may function at stage one level (Proverbs: 22:6 & 15 rob of correction, King Solomon: warning and instruction and correction and teaching his son life stages & GOD's Comments: Old Testament). This learner's parents applied the rod of correction throughout the learner's childhood. This taught the learner right from wrong and about rules and GOD's Comments and about life. In the learner's community, there were family like, grandparents, parents, uncles &aunts.

Issues of race and ethnicity in assessment go beyond the straightforward specifics of language barriers and proficiency. The success of educational methods is to a great extent dependent on cultural factors, and assessment is no different, although in some researches (such as the controversial and widely discredited' Bell Curve' research) cultural issues and prejudices are more marked in the manner of investigation itself rather than any findings (www.sqa.org.uk, Mitch Miller June-July 2005,p38).

The history of race and ethnicity in science and sociology, it need hardly be said that caution must be exercised in looking at this area. In 1992, Secada carried out a much needed and well-balanced study in Mathematics. The chapter discusses the relationship between Mathematics achievement and background factors such as ethnicity, race, language spoken and social class. Among US students, White students do better on standardized achievement tests than Hispanic students, who do slightly better than African American students. The gap in attainment between African American and White students narrows over time on basic skill, but not on higher level skills (http://www.sqa.org.uk ,p38).

OCR's investigation of a complaint against another school district found intentional segregation of African American kindergarten students. Before each school year, the school principal selected approximately 20 African American children from the pool of new kindergarten students and established an all African American class taught by the district's only African American kindergarten teacher. School administrators offered no legitimate nondiscriminatory educational justification for the establishment of the racially segregated class or its assignment to the school's sole African American teacher. Instead, OCR was informed the class was established in response to requests from African American parents and as an attempt to prevent" white flight." The district made commitments to immediately assign students on a basis other than the race of the student or teacher (http://www.ed.gov/about/reports_p2).Major school-integration decisions decided by the U.S.Supreme Court:

1954-Brown v. Board of Education. The Court decides by unanimous rule that racially segregated public schools are unconstitutional and "separate educational facilities are inherently unequal".

1968- Green v. New Kent County, Va., decides that "freedom of choice "plans were ineffective at actually desegregating schools. Supreme Court tells school officials they have a duty to eradicate segregation "root and branch".

1971- Swann v. Charlotte-Mecklenburg Board of Education, N.C. The decision permits busing of students and reforming school district lines to eliminate school segregation. Vincient A. Spears had to walk four miles to High School because in 1972 bus did not pick up blacks.

2007- Parents involved in Community Schools v. Seattle District No.1 and Meredith v.Jefferson County Board of Education. The Court rules against school diversity plans that take students' race into account when determining school assignments (www.buzzle.com/articles/supreme-court/integregation. AT the end of Vincient A. Spears' time travel, he remembers when his younger brother called him an "Uncle Tom "in High School. It is time to put away the name calling that hurts and remember that GOD has no color. Vincient A. Spears works as an

Education and Developmental Aid for Governor Morehead School for the blind where he was asked not to say Merry Christmas at the school. Government worker does not shed one constitutional right to freedom of speech or expression at the gate or building of work (U.S Supreme Court, Tinker v. Des Moines Independent School District, 1969, Know Your Rights, Sekulow Jay Alan, p.20).Students can learn from past history about race relationship from teacher that have to deal with race problems as a way of life in late 1950until the present.

References:

1. Couples 'Devotional Bible, New International Version, Edited by staff of Marriage Partnership magazine.

2.Knowing Your Rights, Sekulow Jay Alan, Copyright 1996, Liberty, Life, and Family Publications.

3.http://www.buzzle.com/articles/sharly-divided-supreme-court-votes-5-4-0n-schools-integregation

4. http://www.sqa.org.uk

5. School Law and the Public Schools, Fourth Edition, Essex Nathan l.,Copyright@2008,2005,2002,1999 Pearson Education, Inc.

6. http://www.sparknotes.com/psychology

7.Excerpts From the Supreme Court Ruling Upholding Busing to End Segregation – article –photo – New York Times (New York NY) – Apr 21, 1971

8.Litigation Push Seen in Ruling – article (NT Times) – News & Observer (Raleigh NC) – Apr 21, 1971

9.Schools Weigh Nixon's Busing Stand – article (AP) -- News & Observer (Raleigh NC) – Aug 5, 1971

10. Mixing without Busing Directed by President – article – Raleigh Times (Raleigh NC) – Aug 11, 1971

11. http://www.news&observer.com/NCSU student apologize for racist graffiti

Stage of life and Rights of Vincient A. Spears

Children need to begin asserting control and power over the environment. Success in this stage of life (Initiative vs. Guilt) leads to sense of purpose (Erikson's Psychosocial Stage of Development). The learner(Vincient A. Spears) traveled back in his time machine when he was 5 year old in 1963 when he past by park car with two young white boys(ages 4 and 5) in it, the learner got near the car and the boys called the learner a" nigger" (Dunn,NC 1963). When the learner got home, the told his parents about what he was call as he walked to downtown. The learner's father said "You are not a nigger but a proud Negro boy and the learner's mother said that "GOD have no color and GOD loves you and created you" and his mother talked about the trial of Jesus: The soldiers led Jesus away into the palace(that is, the Praetorium)and called together the whole company of soldiers. They put a purple robe on him, the twisted together a crown of thorns and set it on him. And they began to call out to him."Hail, king of the Jews (Mark 15:16-20, Holy Bible)!"Again and again they stuck him on the head with a staff and spit on him. Falling on their knees, they paid homage to him. And when they had mocked him, they took off the purple robe and put clothes on him. Then they led him out to crucify him (The New Testament, Holy Bible, p.1095). Then the learner' s father told him about the time he (the father) went to bar with his Army friends and ordered some drinks , the owner came out and said "We do not serve niggers in here". Then , the learner's father said "I am glad you do not serve nigger in here because I do not want a nigger but a beer"(Eugene Spears one the first black male in the Special Force 82nd Airborne). This learner learned about life in the south and civil right. The learner felt guilt about being black and in later years ,the learner remember the song" Said it out loud I' m black and I'm proud" and the movie" Remember The Titan". The learner was taught about GOD and JESUS at a young age and to pray to GOD for help and to talk to the parents about anything, he needs .Children who try to exert too much power experience disapproval, resulting in sense of guilt (Erik Erikson' s Psychosocial Stage of Development). Kohlberg's Moral Development (1963) concepts of consecutive stages are rich with theological implications. Then, Vincient A. Spears traveled to Raleigh, NC on Nov. 5, 2008, when some white students (NCSU) wrote and drew in the University's Free Expression Tunnel:" Let's shoot that n—in the head" and "Hang Obama by a Noose." There also were references to the Ku Klux Klan. U.S Secret Service, which determined the painting were not a serious threat against President-elect Barack Obama's life (Locke Mandy and Friedman Leah, Staff Writers, News& Observer, Nov.20, 2008).But black students did not feel that safe and Vincient A. Spears' a black learner at Strayer University and live in Raleigh, NC , felt that past was repeating itself. Vincient A. Spears got back into the time machine and traveled to Harnett Jr. High School, where a teacher punished him by making him put his nose in circle that was draw on a blackboard. This was cruel and unusual punishment which inflicted such pain of emotions that he could not bear at those times which cause Vincient A. Spears to become quiet and he had to overcome his pain from that punishment. The question of the constitutionality of corporal punishment was reaffirmed in the landmark case Ingraham v.Wright, where the U.S. Supreme Court ruled that even severe corporal punishment may not violate the Eighth Amendment prohibition of cruel and unusual punishment. This case arose when Ingraham and another student from the Dale County, Florida, and public schools filed suit after they had been subjected to paddling. State law allowed corporal punishment if it was not "degrading or unduly severe (School Law and the Public Schools, Fourth Edition, Essex Nathan L.P.76-79) and if it was done after consultation with the principal or other teacher in charge of the school. Paddling was considered a less drastic form of punishment than suspension. For violating a teacher's instruction, Ingraham had received twenty licks while he was held over a table in the principal's office. He required medical attention and missed school for several days. Because this paddling was probably "unduly severe," the high court hearing the evidence and appeals found no constitutional violation. According to Justice Powell," The schoolchild has little need for the protection of the Eighth Amendment." It is more appropriately applied in the case of the criminally convicted and thereby involuntarily confined.

While the court declined to declare corporal punishment as used in the context of public schools to be a violation of the cruel and unusual proscription or due process under federal law, it did state that paddling students deprived them of liberty interests protected by the Constitution. Although not required by law, but in the spirit of fairness, rudimentary due process should be applied before corporal punishment is administered. In spite of the ruling, federal courts have subsequently ruled that excessive corporal punishment violates the substantive due process clause of the Fourteenth Amendment. The courts, however, have fallen short of determining exactly when corporal punishment becomes excessive (p.79).

Although the Ingraham case upholds the legality of corporal punishment as an acceptable means of controlling student behavior, local school district policy in many cases have seriously limited use.

Kohlberg 's theory is especially relevant to current discussions of the gospel (Holy Bible: Four Books of JESUS the CHRIST 's life), the atonement, the Law, Comments and the true character of GOD the father and JESUS the son (John 3:16, Holy Bible).An application of his theory to the story of GOD's dealing with ancient children of Israel, offers a rational explanation of actions on GOD 's part which may seem harsh or unduly severe from our perspective. Stage 1: PUNISHMENT AND OBEDIENCE: Avoidance of physical punishment and deference to power. Punishment is an automatic response of physical retaliation. The immediate physical consequences of an action determine its goodness or badness. The atrocities carried out soldiers during the holocaust who were simply" carrying out orders" under threat of punishment, illustrate that adults as well as children may function at stage one level (Proverbs: 22:6 & 15 rob of correction, King Solomon: warning and instruction and correction and teaching his son life stages & GOD's Comments: Old Testament). This learner's parents applied the rod of correction throughout the learner's childhood. This taught the learner right from wrong and about rules and GOD's Comments and about life. In the learner's community, there were family like, grandparents, parents, uncles &aunts.

Issues of race and ethnicity in assessment go beyond the straightforward specifics of language barriers and proficiency. The success of educational methods is to a great extent dependent on cultural factors, and assessment is no different, although in some researches (such as the controversial and widely discredited' Bell Curve' research) cultural issues and prejudices are more marked in the manner of investigation itself rather than any findings (www.sqa.org.uk, Mitch Miller June-July 2005,p38).

The history of race and ethnicity in science and sociology, it need hardly be said that caution must be exercised in looking at this area. In 1992, Secada carried out a much needed and well-balanced study in Mathematics. The chapter discusses the relationship between Mathematics achievement and background factors such as ethnicity, race, language spoken and social class. Among US students, White students do better on standardized achievement tests than Hispanic students, who do slightly better than African American students. The gap in attainment between African American and White students narrows over time on basic skill, but not on higher level skills (http://www.sqa.org.uk ,p38).

OCR's investigation of a complaint against another school district found intentional segregation of African American kindergarten students. Before each school year, the school principal selected approximately 20 African American children from the pool of new kindergarten students and established an all African American class taught by the district's only African American kindergarten teacher. School administrators offered no legitimate nondiscriminatory educational justification for the establishment of the racially segregated class or its assignment to the school's sole African American teacher. Instead, OCR was informed the class was established in response to requests from African American parents and as an attempt to prevent" white flight." The district made commitments to immediately assign students on a basis other than the race of the student or teacher (http://www.ed.gov/about/reports p2).Major school-integration decisions decided by the U.S.Supreme Court:

1954-Brown v. Board of Education. The Court decides by unanimous rule that racially segregated public schools are unconstitutional and "separate educational facilities are inherently unequal".

1968- Green v. New Kent County, Va., decides that "freedom of choice "plans were ineffective at actually desegregating schools. Supreme Court tells school officials they have a duty to eradicate segregation "root and branch".

1971- Swann v. Charlotte-Mecklenburg Board of Education, N.C. The decision permits busing of students and reforming school district lines to eliminate school segregation. Vincient A. Spears had to walk four miles to High School because in 1972 bus did not pick up blacks.

2007- Parents involved in Community Schools v. Seattle District No.1 and Meredith v.Jefferson County Board of Education. The Court rules against school diversity plans that take students' race into account when determining school assignments (www.buzzle.com/articles/supreme-court/integregation. AT the end of Vincient A. Spears' time travel, he remembers when his younger brother called him an "Uncle Tom "in High School. It is time to put away the name calling that hurts and remember that GOD has no color. Vincient A. Spears works as an Education and Developmental Aid for Governor Morehead School for the blind where he was asked not to say Merry Christmas at the school. Government worker does not shed one constitutional right to freedom of speech or expression at the gate or building of work (U.S Supreme Court, Tinker v. Des Moines Independent School District, 1969, Know Your Rights, Sekulow Jay Alan, p.20).Students can learn from past history about race relationship from teacher that have to deal with race problems as a way of life in late 1950until the present.

References:

1. Couples 'Devotional Bible, New International Version, Edited by staff of Marriage Partnership magazine.

2.Knowing Your Rights, Sekulow Jay Alan, Copyright 1996, Liberty, Life, and Family Publications.

3.http://www.buzzle.com/articles/sharly-divided-supreme-court-votes-5-4-0n-schools-integregation

4. http://www.sqa.org.uk

5. School Law and the Public Schools, Fourth Edition, Essex Nathan l.,Copyright@2008,2005,2002,1999 Pearson Education, Inc.

6. http://www.sparknotes.com/psychology

7.Excerpts From the Supreme Court Ruling Upholding Busing to End Segregation – article –photo – New York Times (New York NY) – Apr 21, 1971

8.Litigation Push Seen in Ruling – article (NT Times) – News & Observer (Raleigh NC) – Apr 21, 1971

9.Schools Weigh Nixon's Busing Stand – article (AP) -- News & Observer (Raleigh NC) – Aug 5, 1971

10. Mixing without Busing Directed by President – article – Raleigh Times (Raleigh NC) – Aug 11, 1971

11. http://www.news&observer.com/NCSU student apologize for racist graffiti

Computers as Mindtools for Engaging Critical Thinking and Representing Knowledge
David Jonassen Pennsylvania State University, USA

jonassen@psu.edu

Introduction

Traditionally, instructional technologies have been used as media for conveying information, much as teachers do. When used in this way, information is "stored" in the technology. During the "instructional" process, learners interpret the messages stored in the technology as they "interact" it. However, those interactions are very limited. The technology program judges the learner's response and provides feedback about how accurately the learners' responses resembled what was presented to them. Learning is limited to the acquisition and repetition of information. Such learning is not meaningful. Using computers to "teach" students in this traditional way is not appropriate because it does not mindfully engage students in making meaning.

In this paper, I argue that technologies should not support learning by attempting to instruct the learners, but rather should be used as knowledge construction and representation tools that students learn *with*, not *from*. In this way, learners function as designers, and the computers function as Mindtools for helping learners to interpret and organize their personal knowledge.

Mindtools are computer applications that, when used by learners to represent what they know, necessarily engage them in critical thinking about the content they are studying (Jonassen, 1996). Mindtools scaffold different forms of reasoning about the content that students are studying. That is, they require students to think about what they know in different, meaningful ways. For instance, using databases to organize students' understanding of content organization necessarily engages them in analytical reasoning, where creating an expert system rule base requires them to think about the causal relationships between ideas. Students cannot use Mindtools as learning strategies without thinking deeply about what they are studying.

Using Computers as Mindtools

Mindtools repurpose computer applications to engage learners in critical thinking. There are several classes of Mindtools, including semantic organization tools, dynamic modeling tools, information interpretation tools, knowledge construction tools, and conversation and collaboration tools (Jonassen, in press). I shall briefly describe and illustrate some of them. For a report of research on Mindtools, see Jonassen and Reeves (1996).

Semantic Organization Tools

Semantic organization tools help learners to analyze and organize what they know or what they are learning. Two of the best known semantic organization tools are databases and semantic networking (concept mapping) tools.

Databases. Database management systems are computerized record keeping systems that were developed originally to replace paper-based filing systems. These electronic filing cabinets allow users to store information in organized databases that facilitates retrieval. Content is broken down into records that are divided into fields which describe the kind of information in different parts of each record.

Databases can be used as tools for analyzing and organizing subject matter (i.e. Mindtools). The database shown in Figure 1 was developed by students studying cells and their functions in a biology course. The database can then be searched and sorted to answer specific questions about the content or to identify interrelationships and inferences from the content, such as "Do different shaped cells have specific functions?" Constructing content databases requires learners to develop a data structure, locate relevant information, insert it in appropriate fields and records, and search and sort the database to answer content queries. A large number of critical thinking skills are required to use and construct knowledge-oriented databases.

cell type	location	function	shape	tissue systems	specialization	related cell
Astocyte	CNS	Supply Nutrients	Radiating	Nervous	Half of Neural Tissue	Neurons, Capillaries
Basal	Stratum Basale	Produce New Cells	Cube, Columnar	Epithelial	Mitotic	Epithelial Cells
Basophils	Blood Plasma	Bind Imm. I	Lobed Nuclei	Connective, Immune	Basic, Possible Mast	Neutrophil, Eosinophil
Cardiac Muscle	Heart	Pump Blood	Branched	Muscle	Intercalated discs	Endomysium
Chondroblast	Cartilage	Produce Matrix	Round	Connective		
Eosinophil	Blood Plasma	Protazoans, Allergy	Two Lobes	Connective, Immune	Acid, Phagocytes (Prote	Basophil, Neutrophil
Ependymal	Line CNS	Form Cerebralspinal Fluid	Cube	Nervous	Cilia	
Erythrocytes	Blood Plasma	Transport O2, Remove CO2	Disc	Connective	Transport	Hemocytoblast, Proeryt
Fibroblast	Connective Tissue	Fiber Production	Flat, Branched	Connective	Mitotic	
Goblet	Columnar Epithelial	Secretion	Columnar	Epithelial	Mucus	Columnar
Keratinocytes	Stratum Basal	Strengthen other Cells	Round	Epithelial		Melanocytes
Melanocytes	Stratum Basale	U.V. Protection	Branched	Epithelial	Produce Melanin	Keratinocytes
Microglia	CNS	Protect	Ovoid	Nervous	Macrophage	Neurons, Astrocytes?
Motor Neuron	CNS (Cell Body)	Impulse Away from CNS	Long, Thin	Nervous	Multipolar, Neuromuscul	Sensory Neuron, Neurog
Neutrophil	Blood Plasma	Inflammation, Bacteria	Lobed Nuclei	Connective, Immune	Phagocytos, Neutral	Basophils, Eosinophil
Oligodendrocyte	CNS	Insulate	Long	Nervous	Produce Myaline Sheath	Neurons
Osteoblast	Bone	Produce Organic Matrix	Spider	Connective	Bone Salts	Osteoclasts
Osteoclast	Bone	Bone Restoration	Ruffled Boarder	Connective	Destroy Bone	Osteoblasts
Pseudostratified	Gland Ducts, Respira	Secretion	Varies	Epithelial	Cilia	Goblet

Figure 1. Content database.

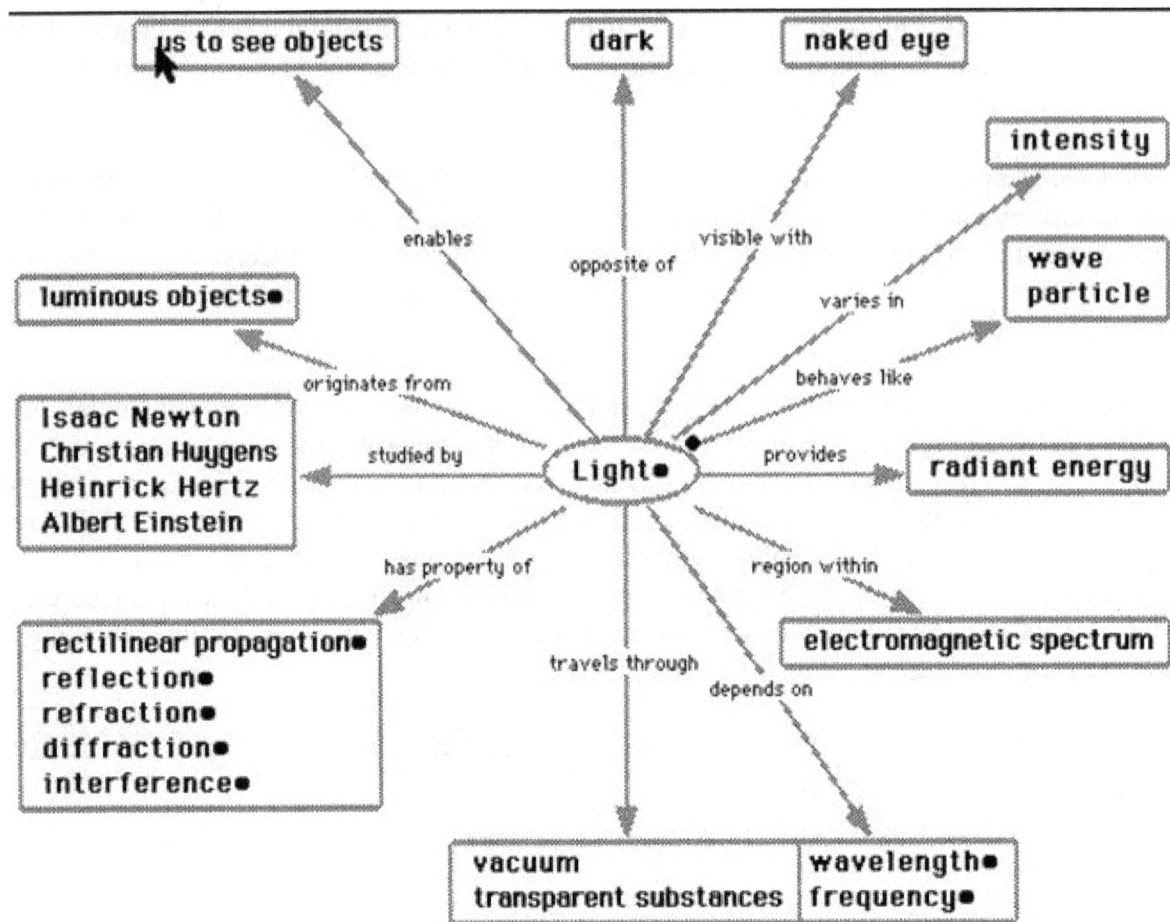

Figure 2. Semantic network. **Semantic Networking**. Semantic networking tools provide visual screen tools for producing concept maps. Concept mapping is a study strategy that requires learners to draw visual maps of concepts connected to each other via lines (links). These maps are spatial representations of ideas and their interrelationships that are stored in memory, i.e. structural knowledge (Jonassen, Beissner, & Yacci, 1993). Semantic networking programs are computer-based, visualizing tools for developing representations of semantic networks in memory. Programs such as SemNet, Learning Tool, Inspriation, Mind Mapper, and many others, enable learners to interrelate the ideas that they are studying in multidimensional networks of concepts, to label the relationships between those concepts, and to describe the nature of the relationships between all of the ideas in the network, such as that in Figure 2.

The purpose of semantic networks is to represent the structure of knowledge that someone has constructed. So, creating semantic networks requires learners to analyze the structural relationships among the content they are studying. By comparing semantic networks created at different points in time, they can also be used as evaluation tools for assessing changes in thinking by learners. If we agree that is a semantic network is a meaningful representations of memory, then learning from this perspective can be thought of as a reorganization of semantic memory. Producing semantic networks reflect those changes in semantic memory, since the networks describe what learners know. So, semantic networking programs can be use to reflect the process of knowledge construction.

Dynamic Modeling Tools

While semantic organization tools help learners to represent the semantic relationships among ideas, dynamic modeling tools help learners to describe the dynamic relationships among ideas. Dynamic modeling tools include spreadsheets, expert systems, systems modeling tools, and microworlds, among others.

Spreadsheets. Spreadsheets are computerized, numerical record keeping systems that were designed originally to replace paper-based, ledger accounting systems. Essentially, a spreadsheet is a grid or matrix of empty cells with columns identified by letters and rows identified by numbers. Each cell is a placeholder for values, formulas relating values in other cells, or functions that mathematically or logically manipulate values in other cells. Functions are small programmed sequences that may, for instance, match values in cells with other cells, look up a variable in a table of values, or create an index of values to be compared with other cells.

Spreadsheets were originally developed and are most commonly used to support business decision making and accounting operations. They are especially useful for answering "what if" questions, for instance, what if interest rates increased by one percent? Changes made in one cell automatically recalculate all of the affected values in other cells. Spreadsheets are also commonly used for personal accounting and budgeting.

Spreadsheets also may be used as Mindtools for amplifying mental functioning. In the same way that they have qualitatively changed the accounting process, spreadsheets can change the educational process when working with quantitative information. Spreadsheets model the mathematical logic that is implied by calculations. Making the underlying logic obvious to learners should improve their understanding of the interrelationships and procedures. Numerous educators have explored the use of spreadsheets as Mindtools. Spreadsheets have frequently been used in mathematics classes to calculate quantitative relationships in various chemistry and physics classes. They are also useful in social studies instruction and have even supported ecology. Spreadsheets are flexible Mindtools for representing, reflecting on, and calculating quantitative information. Building spreadsheets requires abstract reasoning by the user, they are rule-using tools that require that users become rule-makers. Spreadsheets also support problem solving activities, such decision analysis reasoning requires learners to consider implications of conditions or options, which requires entails higher order reasoning.

Expert Systems. Expert systems have evolved from research in the field of artificial intelligence. An expert system is a computer program that simulates the way human experts solve problems, that is, an artificial decision maker. They are computer-based tools that are designed to function as intelligent decision supports. For example, expert systems have been developed to help geologists decide where to drill for oil, bankers to evaluate loan application, computer sales technicians how to configure computer systems, and employees to decide among a large number of company benefits alternatives. Problems whose solutions require decision making are good candidates for expert system development.

Most expert systems consist of several components, including the knowledge base, inference engine, and user interface. There are a variety of "shells" or editors for creating expert system knowledge bases, which is the part of the activity that engages the critical thinking. Building the knowledge base requires the learner to articulate causal knowledge.

The development of expert systems results in deeper understanding because they provide an intellectual environment that demands the refinement of domain knowledge, supports problem solving, and monitors the acquisition of knowledge. A good deal of research has focused on developing expert system advisors to help teachers identify and classify learning disabled students.

Systems Modeling Tools. Complex learning requires students to solve complex and ill-structured problems as well as simple problems. Complex learning requires that students

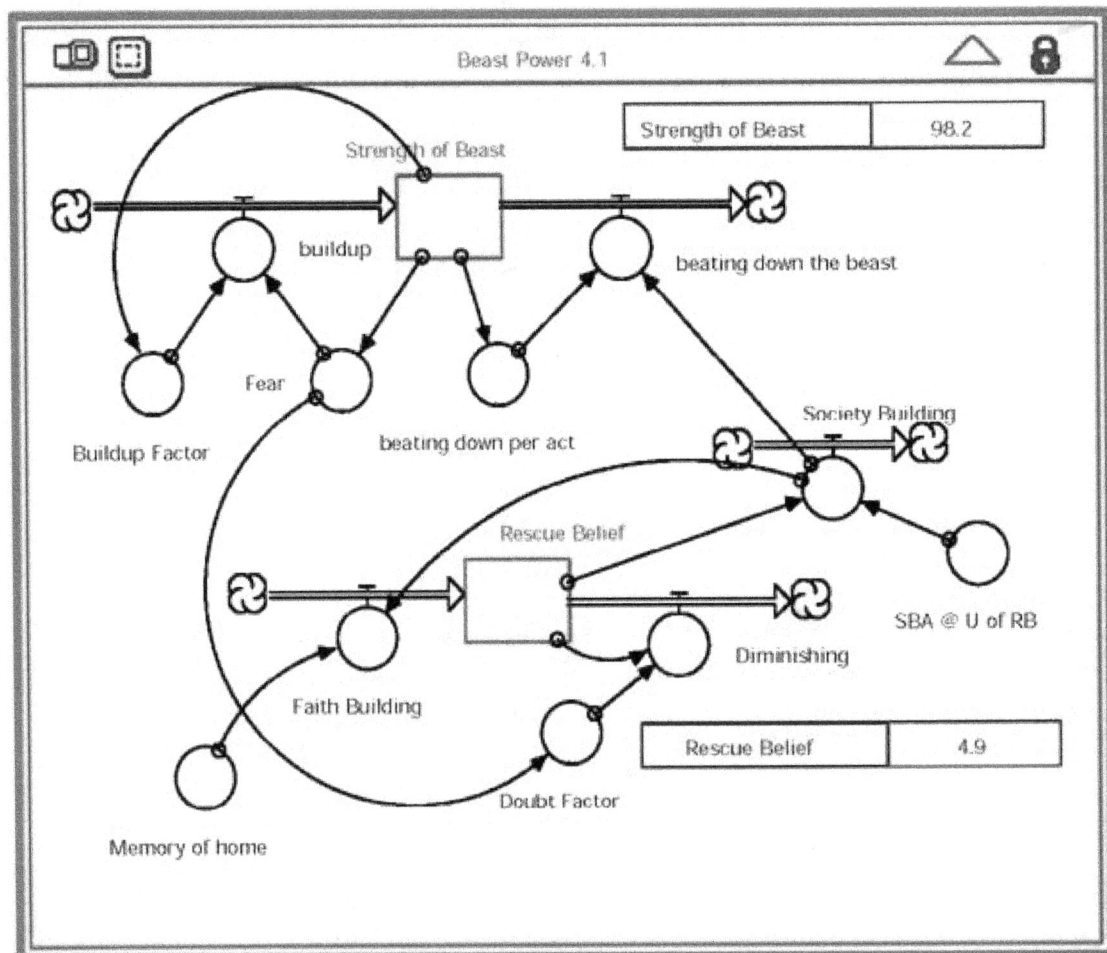

Fig. 4. Conceptual map of the Beast.

develop complex mental representations of the phenomena they are studying. A number of tools for developing these mental representations are emerging. Stella, for instance, is a powerful and flexible tool for building simulations of dynamic systems and processes (systems with interactive and interdependent components). Stella uses a simple set of building block icons to construct a map of a process (see Fig. 4). The Stella model in Fig. 4 was developed by an English teacher in conjunction with his tenth grade students to describing how the boys' loss of hope drives the increasing power of the beast in William Golding's novel, *The Lord of the Flies*. The model of beast power represent the factors that contributed to the strength of the beast in the book, including fear and resistance. Each component can be opened up, so that values for each component may be stated as constants or variables. Variables can be stated as equations containing numerical relationships among any of the variables connected to it. The resulting model can be run, changing the values of faith building, fear, and memory of home experienced by the boys while assessing the effects on their belief about being rescued and the strength of the beast within them. Stella and other dynamic modeling tools, such as Model-It from the Highly Interactive Computing Group at the University of Michigan, probably provides the most complete intellectual activity that students can engage in.

Microworlds. Microworlds are exploratory learning environments or discovery spaces, in which learners can navigate, manipulate or create objects, and test their effects on one another. Microworlds contain constrained simulations of real-world phenomena that allow learners to control those phenomena. They provide the exploratory functionality (provide learners with the observation and manipulation tools and testing objects) needed to explore phenomena in those parts of the world. Video-based adventure games are microworlds that require players to master each environment before moving onto more complex environments. They are compelling to youngsters, who spend hours transfixed in these adventure worlds. Microworlds are perhaps the ultimate example of active learning environments, because the users can exercise so much control over the environment.

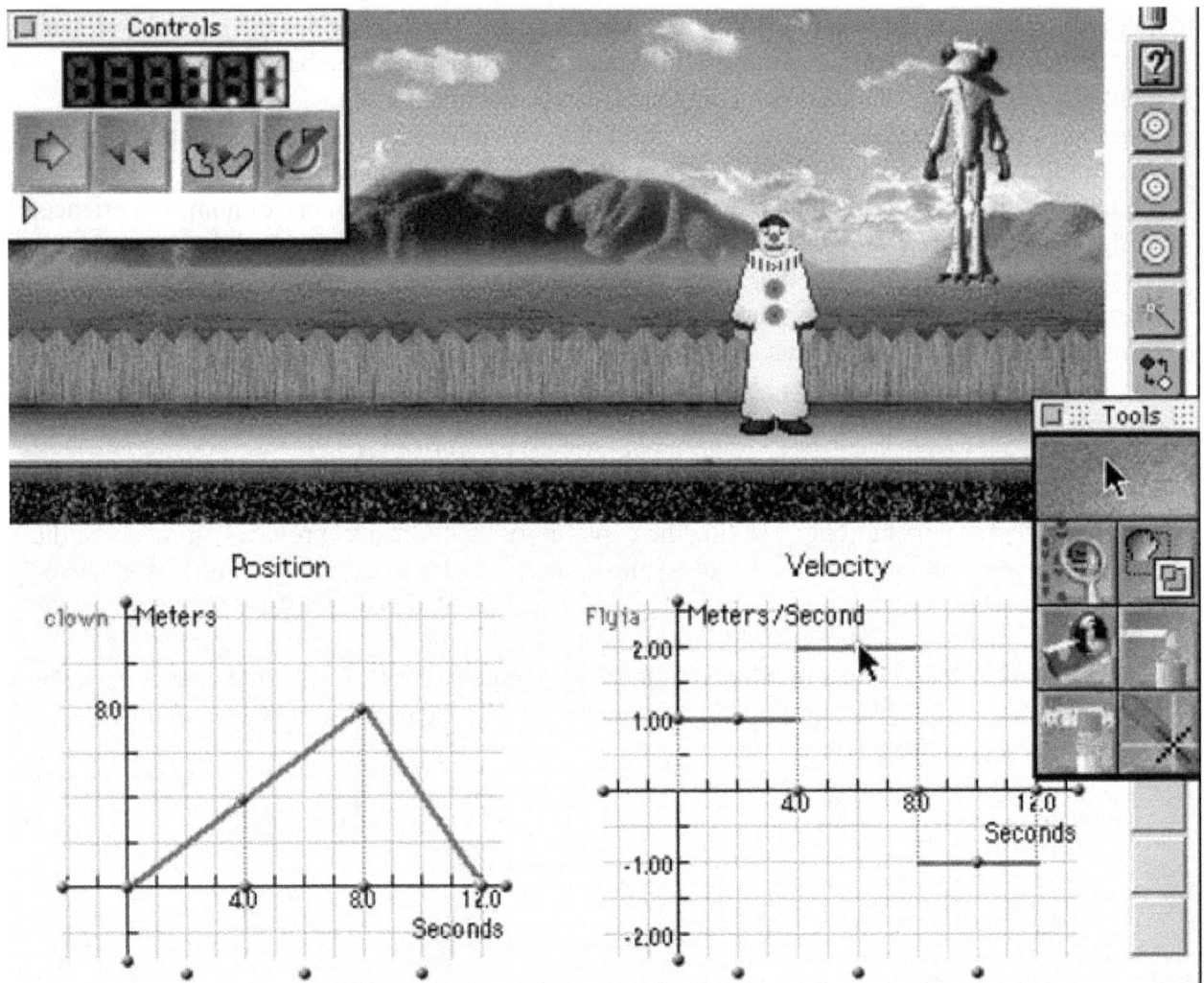

Fig.5. Experiment in Math World..

Many microworlds are being produced and made available from educational research projects, especially in math and science. In mathematics, the Geometric Supposer and Algebraic Supposer are standard tools for testing conjectures in geometry and algebra by constructing and manipulating geometric and algebraic objects in order to explore the relationships within and between these objects (Yerulshamy & Schwartz, 1986). The emphasis in those microworlds is the generation and testing of hypotheses. They provide a testbed for testing students' predictions about geometric and algebraic proofs.

The SimCalc project teaches middle and high school students calculus concepts through MathWorlds, which is a microworld consisting of animated worlds and dynamic graphs in which actors move according to graphs. By exploring the movement of the actors in the simulations and seeing the graphs of their activity, students begin to understand important calculus ideas. In the MathWorlds activity illustrated in Fig. 5, students match two motions. By matching two motions they learn how velocity and position graphs relate. Students must match the motion of the green and red graphs. To do this, they can change either graph. They iteratively run the simulation to see if you got it right! Students may also use MathWorld's link to enter their own bodily motion.

For example, a student can walk across the classroom, and their motions would be entered into MathWorlds through sensing equipment. MathWorld would plot their motion, enabling the students to explore the properties of their own motion.

Information Interpretation Tools

The volume and complexity of information are growing at an astounding rate. Learners need tools that help them to access and process that information. A new class of intelligent information search engines are scanning information resources, like the World Wide Web, and locating relevant resources for learners. Other tools, for helping learners make sense of what they find, are also emerging.

Visualization Tools. We take in more information through our visual modality than any other sensory system, yet we cannot output ideas visually, except in mental images and dreams, which cannot be shared visually except using paint/draw programs. While it is not yet possible to dump our mental images directly from our brains into a computer, a very new and growing class of visualization tools are mediating this process by providing us tools that allow us to reason visually in certain areas. Visualization tools help humans to represent and convey those mental images, usually not in the same form they are generated mentally, but as rough approximations of those mental images.

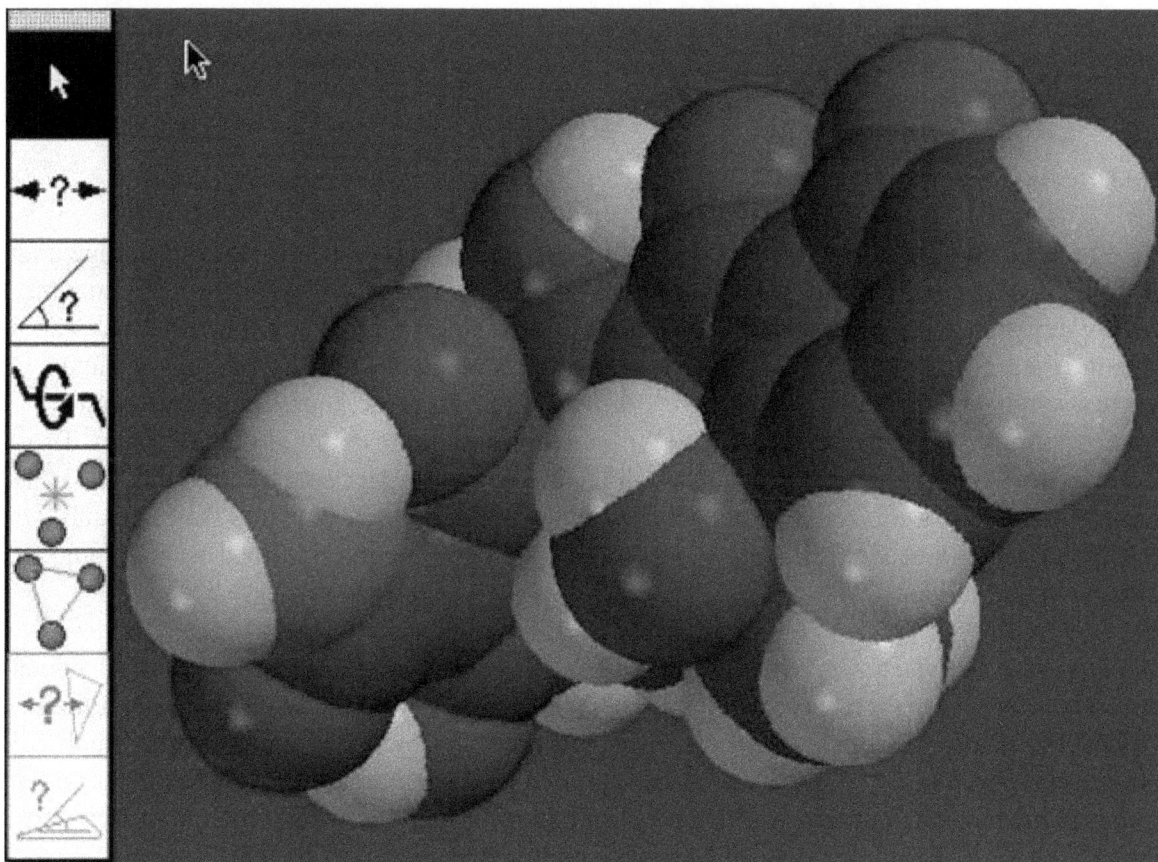

Fig 6. Tool for visualizing chemical compounds.

Visualization tools can have two major uses, interpretive and expressive (Gordin, Edelson & Gomez, 1996). Interpretive tools help learners view and manipulate visuals, extracting meaning from the information being visualized. Interpretive illustrations help to clarify difficult-to-understand text and abstract concepts, making them more comprehensible (Levin, Anglin, & Carney, 1995). Expressive visualization helps learners to visually convey meaning in order to communicate a set of beliefs. Crayons and paper or paint and draw programs are powerful expressive tools that learners use to express themselves visually. However, they rely on graphical talent. Visualization tools go beyond paint and draw programs by scaffolding or supporting some of the expression, They help learners to visualize ideas in ways that make them more easily interpretable by other viewers. An excellent example of an expressive visualization tool is the growing number of tools for visualizing chemical compounds. Understanding chemical bonding is difficult for most people, because the complex atomic interactions are not visible. Static graphics of these bonds found in textbooks may help learners to form mental images, but those mental images are not manipulable and cannot be conveyed to others. Tools such as MacSpartan enables students to view, rotate, and measure molecules using different views (see Fig. 6) and also to modify or construct new molecules. These visualization tools make the abstract real for students, helping them to understand chemical concepts that are difficult to convey in static displays.

Knowledge Construction Tools

Papert has used the term "constructionism" to describe the process of knowledge construction resulting from constructing things. When learners function as designers of objects, they learn more about those objects than they would from studying about them.

Hypermedia

Hypermedia consists of information nodes, which are the basic unit of information storage and may consist of a page of text, a graphic, a sound bite, a video clip, or even an entire document. In many hypermedia systems, nodes can be amended or modified by the user. The user may add to or change the information in a node or create his or her own nodes of information, so that a hypertext can be a dynamic knowledge base that continues to grow, representing new and different points of view. Nodes are made accessible through links that interconnect them. The links in hypermedia transport the user through the information space to the nodes that are selected, enabling the user to navigate through the knowledge base. The node structure and the link structure form a network of ideas in the knowledge base, the interrelated and interconnected group or system of ideas.

While hypermedia systems have traditionally been used as information retrieval systems which learners browse, learners may create their own hypermedia knowledge bases that reflect their own understanding of ideas. Students are likely to learn more by constructing instructional materials than by studying them. Designing multimedia presentations is a complex process that engages many skills in learners, and it can be applied to virtually any content domain. Carver, Lehrer, Connell, & Ericksen (1992) list some of the major thinking skills that learners need to use as designers, including project management skills, research skills, organization and representation skills, presentation skills, and reflection skills.

Conversation Tools

Newer theories of learning are emphasizing the social as well as the constructivist nature of the learning process. In real world settings, we often learn by socially negotiating meaning, not by being taught. A variety of synchronous and asynchronous computer-supported environments are available for supporting this social negotiation process. Online telecommunications include live conversations, such as Chats, MOOs, and MUDs and videoconferencing, and asynchronous discussions, including electronic mail, Listservs, bulletin boards, and computer conferences. These many forms of telecommunications can be used for supporting interpersonal exchanges among students, collecting information, and solving problems in groups of students (Jonassen, Peck, & Wilson, 1998).Interpersonal exchanges may include keypals, global classrooms, electronic appearances, electronic mentoring, and impersonations (Harris, 1995). Examples of information collections include information exchanges, database creation, electronic publishing, electronic field trips, and pooled data analysis. Problem-solving projects include information searches, parallel problem solving, electronic process writing, serial creations, simulations, and social action projects.

Online communication presumes that students can communicate, that is, that they can meaningfully participate in conversations. In order to do that, they need to be able to interpret messages, consider appropriate responses, and construct coherent replies. Many students are not able to engage in cogent and coherent discourse. Why? Because, most students have rarely been asked to contribute their opinions about topics. They have been too busy memorizing what the teachers tell them. So, it may be necessary to support students' attempts to converse. A number of online communication environments have been designed to support students' discourse skills, such as the Collaboratory Notebook (O'Neill & Gomez, 1994). The Collaboratory Notebook is a collaborative hypermedia composition system designed to support within- and cross-school science projects. What is unique about the Collaboratory is that it focuses on project investigations rather than curricular content. During a project, the teacher or any student can pose a question or a conjecture (Fig. 6), which can be addressed by participants from around the country. The Collaboratory provides a scaffolding structure for conversations by requiring specific kinds of responses to messages. For instance, in order to support the conjecture in Fig. 6, learners can only "provide evidence" or "develop a plan" to support that conjecture. This form of scaffolded conversation results in more coherent and cogent conversations.

Title: Does pollution affect the weather?

Authors: covis

Page Contents: Text ▼

The Greenhouse Effect has resulted from holes in the ozone layer. These holes have resulted from chemical reactions caused by inductrial pollutants.

Page type:

This page is a conjecture

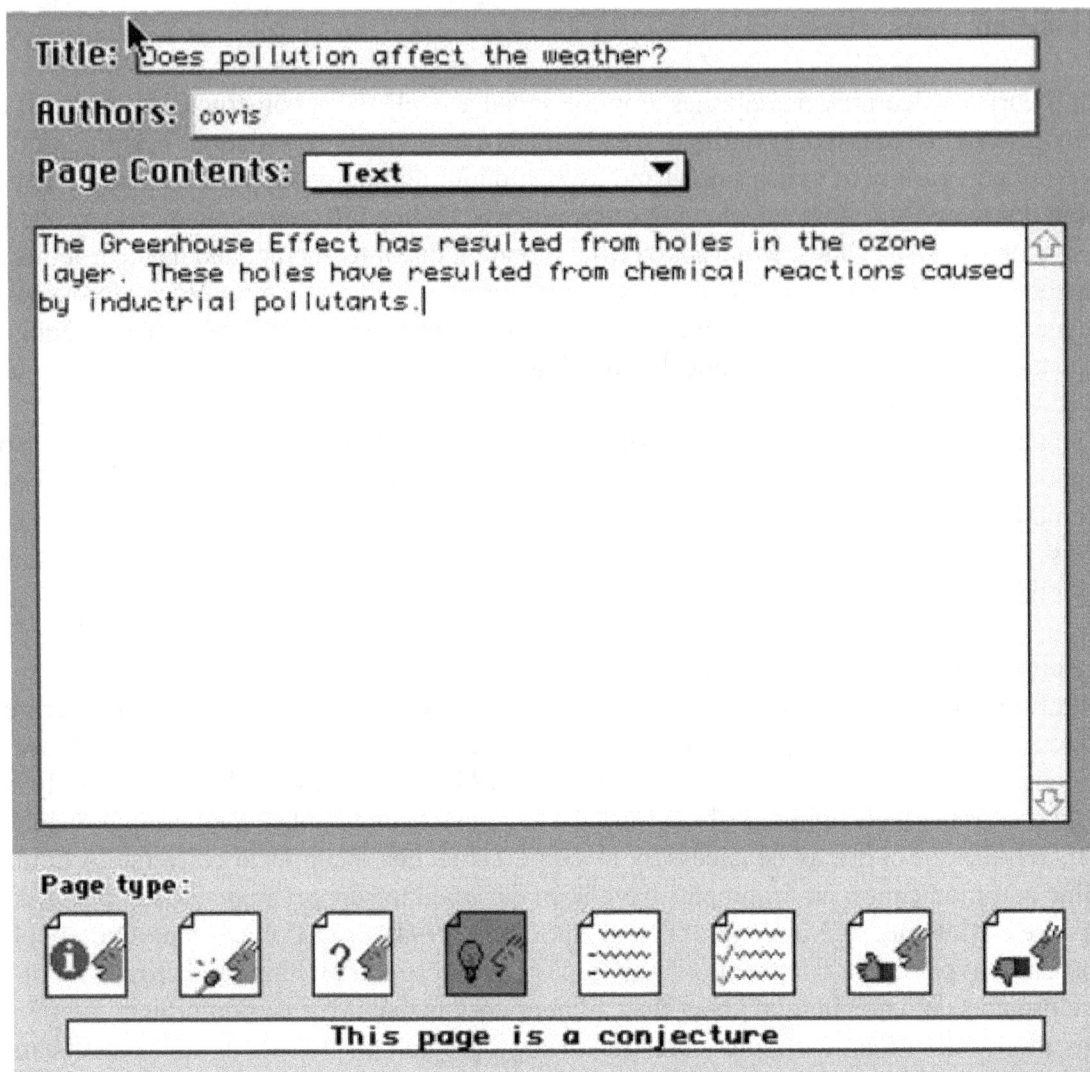

Collaborative conversations are becoming an increasingly popular way to support socially co-constructed learning. Many more sophisticated computer-supported conferencing environments are becoming available to support learner conversations.

Rationales for Using Technology as Mindtools

Why do Mindtools work, that is, why do they engage learners in critical, higher-order thinking about content?

Learners as Designers

The people who learn the most from designing instructional materials are the designers, not the learners for whom the materials are intended. The process of articulating what we know in order to construct a knowledge base forces learners to reflect on what they are studying in new and meaningful ways. The common homily, "the quickest way to learn about something is to have to teach it,"explains the effectiveness of Mindtools, because learners are teaching the computer. It is important to emphasize that Mindtools are not intended necessarily to make learning easier.

Learners do not use Mindtools naturally and effortlessly. Rather, Mindtools often require learners to think harder about the subject matter domain being studied while generating thoughts that would be impossible without the tool. While they are thinking harder, learners are also thinking more meaningfully as they construct their own realities by designing their own knowledge bases.

Knowledge Construction, Not Reproduction

Mindtools represent a constructivist use of technology. Constructivism is concerned with the process of how we *construct* knowledge. When students develop databases, for instance, they are constructing their own conceptualization of the organization of a content domain. How we construct knowledge depends upon we already know, which depends on the kinds of experiences that we have had, how we have organized those experiences into knowledge structures, and what we believe about what we know. So, the meaning that each of us makes for an experience resides in the mind of each knower. This does not mean that we can comprehend *only* our own interpretation of reality. Rather, learners are able to comprehend a variety of interpretations and to use each in constructing personal knowledge.

Constructivist approaches to learning strive to create environments where learners actively participate in the environment in ways that are intended to help them construct their own knowledge, rather than having the teacher interpret the world and insure that students understand the world as they have told them. In constructivist environments, like Mindtools, learners are actively engaged in interpreting the external world and reflecting on their interpretations. This is not "active" in the sense that learners actively listen and then mirror the *one* correct view of reality, but rather "active" in the sense that learners must participate and interact with the surrounding environment in order to create their own view of the subject. Mindtools function as formalisms for guiding learners in the organization and representation of what they know.

Learning *with* Technology

The primary distinction between computers as tutors and computers as Mindtools is best expressed by Salomon, Perkins, and Globerson (1991) as the effects *of* technology versus the effects *with* computer technology. Learning *with* computers refers to the learner entering an intellectual partnership with the computer. Learning *with* Mindtools depends "on the mindful engagement of learners in the tasks afforded by these tools and that there is the possibility of qualitatively upgrading the performance of the joint system of learner plus technology." In other words, when students work with computer technologies, instead of being controlled by them, they enhance the capabilities of the computer, and the computer enhances their thinking and learning. The result of an intellectual partnership with the computer is that the whole of learning becomes greater than the sum of its parts. Electronics specialists use their tools to solve problems. The tools do not control the specialist. Neither should computers control learning. Rather, computers should be used as tools that help learners to build knowledge.

(UN) intelligent Tools

Educational communications too often try to do the thinking for learners, to act like tutors and guide the learning. These systems possess some degree of "intelligence" that they use to make instructional decisions about how much and what kind of instruction learners need. Derry and LaJoie (1993) argue that "the appropriate role for a computer system is not that of a teacher/expert, but rather, that of a mind-extension "cognitive tool" (p. 5). Mindtools are *un*intelligent tools, relying on the learner to provide the intelligence, not the computer. This means that planning, decision-making, and self-regulation of learning are the responsibility of the learner, not the computer. However, computer systems can serve as powerful catalysts for facilitating these skills assuming they are used in ways that promote reflection, discussion, and problem solving.

Distributing Cognitive Processing

Computer tools, unlike most tools, can function as intellectual partners which share the cognitive burden of carrying out tasks (Salomon, 1993). When learners use computers as partners, they off-load some of the unproductive memorizing tasks to the computer, allowing the learner to think more productively. Our goal as technology-using educators should be to allocate to the learners the cognitive responsibility for the processing they do best while requiring the technology to do the processing that it does best. Rather than using the limited capabilities of the computer to present information and judge learner input (neither of which computers do well) while asking learners to memorize information and later recall it (which computers do with far greater speed and accuracy than humans), we should assign cognitive responsibility to the part of the learning system that does it the best. Learners should be responsible for recognizing and judging patterns of information and then organizing it, while the computer system should perform calculations, store, and retrieve information. When used as Mindtools, we are engaging learners in the kinds or processing that they do best.

Cost and Effort Beneficial

Mind tools are personal knowledge construction tools that can be applied to any subject matter domain. For the most part, Mind tools software is readily available and affordable. Many computers come bundled with the software described in this paper. Most other applications are in the public domain or available for less than $100. Mind tools are also reasonably easy to learn. The level of skill needed to use Mind tools often requires limited study. Most can be mastered within a couple of hours. Because they can be used to construct knowledge in nearly any course, the cost and learning effort are even more reasonable.

Summary

Computers can most effectively support meaningful learning and knowledge construction in higher education as cognitive amplification tools for reflecting on what students have learned and what they know. Rather than using the power of computer technologies to disseminate information, they should be used in all subject domains as tools for engaging learners in reflective, critical thinking about the ideas they are studying. Using computers as Mindtools by employing software applications as knowledge representation formalisms will facilitate meaning making more readily and more completely than the computer-based instruction now available.

This paper has introduced the concept of Mind tools and provided brief descriptions and some examples. More information and examples are available on the World Wide Web (http://www.ed.psu.edu/~mindtools/).

References

Carver, S.M., Lehrer, R., Connell, T., & Ericksen, J. (1992). Learning by hypermedia design: Issues of assessment and implementation. *Educational Psychologist, 27* (3), 385-404.

Derry, S.J., & LaJoie, S.P. (1993). A middle camp for (un)intelligent instructional computing: An introduction. In S.P. LaJoie & S.J. Derry (Eds.), *Computers as cognitive tools* (pp. 1-14). Hillsdale, NJ: Lawrence Erlbaum Associates.

Gordin, D. N., Edelson, D. C., & Gomez, L. (July, 1996). Scientific visualization as an interpretive and expressive medium. In. D. Edelson & E. Domeshek (Eds.), Proceedings of the Second International Conference on the learning Sciences (pp. 409414). Charlottesville, VA: Association for the Advancement of Computers in Education.

Harris, J. (1995, February). Organizing and facilitating telecollaborative projects. *The Computing Teacher*, 22 (5), 66-69. [Online document: http://www.ed.uiuc.edu/Mining/February95-TCT.html]

Jonassen, D.H. (1996). *Computers in the classroom: Mindtools for critical thinking.* Columbus, OH: Merrill/Prentice-Hall.

Jonassen, D.H. (in press). *Mindtools for engaging critical thinking in the classroom*, 2nd Ed. Columbus, OH: Prentice-Hall.

Jonassen, D.H., Beissner, K., & Yacci, M.A. (1993). *Structural knowledge: Techniques for representing, assessing, and acquiring structural knowledge.* Hillsdale, NJ: Lawrence Erlbaum Associates.

Jonassen, D.H., Peck, K.L., & Wilson, B.G. (1998). *Learning WITH technology: A constructivist perspective.* Columbus, OH: Prentice-Hall.

Jonassen, D.H., & Reeves, T. C. (1996). Learning with technology: Using computers as cognitive tools. In D.H. Jonassen (Ed.), *Handbook of research for educational communications and technology* (pp. 693-719). New York: Macmillan.

O'Neill, D. K., & Gomez, L. M. (1992). The Collaboratory notebook: A distributed knowledge building environment for project learning. Proceedings of ED MEDIA, 94. Vancouver B. C., Canada.

Perkins, D.N. (1986). *Knowledge as design*. Hillsdale, NJ: Lawrence Erlbaum.

Salomon, G. , Perkins, D.N., & Globerson, T. (1991). Partners in cognition: Extending human intelligence with intelligent technologies. *Educational Researcher, 20*(3), 2-9.

Yerulshamy, M., & Schwartz, J. (1986). The geometric supposer: Promoting thinking and learning. *Mathematics Teacher, 79*, 418-422.

Contents

RESEARCH PAPER: USING TECHNOLOGY TO TECH FETAL Alcohol Syndrome/ Fetal

Alcohol Effect

INVESTIGATING EFFECTENESS OF THE LAW "NO CHILD